JOHN OF THE CROSS:
THE LIVING FLAME
OF LOVE

LEONARD DOOHAN

For my wife, Helen, on the occasion of our fortieth
wedding anniversary, with all my love.

ISBN 978-0991006755

ISBN 0991006755

The Author

Dr. Leonard Doohan is Professor Emeritus at Gonzaga University where he was a professor of religious studies for 27 years and Dean of the Graduate School for 13 years. He has written 24 books and many articles and has given over 350 workshops throughout the US, Canada, Europe, Australia, New Zealand, and the Far East. Leonard's recent books include *Spiritual Leadership: the Quest for Integrity*, published by Paulist Press in 2007, *Enjoying Retirement: Living Life to the Fullest*, published by Paulist Press in 2010, *Courageous Hope: The Call of Leadership*, published by Paulist Press in 2011, and The *One Thing Necessary: The Transforming Power of Christian Love*, published by ACTA Publications in 2012.

Dr. Doohan has given courses and workshops on John of the Cross all over the world and his published tapes have been used throughout the English speaking countries.

This current book is the fourth in a new series that explores the major works of John of the Cross for the non-specialist, presenting all the needed background to appreciate this wonderful spiritual writer.

Books on John of the Cross by Leonard Doohan.

The Contemporary Challenge of John of the Cross

John of the Cross: Your Spiritual Guide

The Dark Night is Our Only Light: A study of the
book of the *Dark Night* by John of the Cross

The Spiritual Canticle: The Encounter of Two Lovers.
An introduction to the book of the *Spiritual
Canticle* by John of the Cross

John of the Cross: The Living Flame of Love

ABBREVIATIONS OF THE WORKS OF JOHN OF THE
CROSS

A = Ascent of Mount Carmel
N = Dark Night
C= Spiritual Canticle
F = Living Flame
P = Poetry
S = Sayings of Light and Love
Pr = Precautions
L = Letters

Table of contents

INTRODUCTION

When I was young I loved to go to North Wales and the region around Mount Snowdon, or to the English Lake District with its mountains. I would look up to what seemed great heights—they were actually only hills—and I told myself "I want to get there." Later, when I studied glaciation in the Valle d'Aosta—the Northwest region of Italy—I would look up to Gran Paradiso, Monte Rosa, the Matterhorn, and other great peaks, and I longed to be up there! At one time or another as I grew older I reached all the hilltops of England and Wales and some of the peaks of the Alps. The climb may well be exhausting but when you reach the goal of your climb you feel on top of the world in more ways than one. When you see things from the perspective of the mountaintop everything changes and you see the valleys below, the world, other people, and yourself in different ways. Moreover, only when you have reached the summit does all your training, exhaustion, sacrifices, and endurance seem to have been worthwhile. Many balk at the training that is needed and they never get to the top. Others might use a helicopter or a ski-lift but they never feel the same nor appreciate the sense of celebration that only comes after intense, prolonged, commitment. Moreover, the more difficult the climb, the greater the need of a good, reliable, knowledgeable, experienced guide. No climber who has been to the top thinks about the training and sacrifice that were needed. He or she only concentrates on the thrill, joy, and enrichment of a vision that gives new meaning to life. When a climber arrives at the top, he or she is generally filled with awe and peaceful satisfaction. All climbers know that the experience of arriving at the top of the world motivates you in all you do.

The *Living Flame of Love* describes the goal, the peak of the spiritual journey. Everything else about the journey gets its meaning from this encounter. It is the final part of John's vision of the spiritual life. The *Ascent* and the *Dark Night* led us through the journey of faith and the purifications of sense and spirit needed to lead to union. The *Spiritual Canticle* described the journey of love from early longings to betrothal and spiritual marriage. The *Living Flame* presents four aspects of the final stage in spiritual life—spiritual marriage. It is not itself a further stage in spiritual life but a deeper appreciation of the transformation experienced in spiritual marriage and of the quality of love that becomes more intensified at this time. This is a book for everyone including those who have not reached these later stages of spiritual life, for its vision fills readers with enthusiasm for the goal and with motivation for the journey.

This short book gives the appropriate background for understanding John's spiritual masterpiece. Chapter one looks at John's vision of love. Chapter two looks at all the preparatory stages to get to the summit—teachings that John gives in three digressions to the first three stanzas. Chapter three introduces us to the *Living Flame*, both poem and commentary, and its relationship to John's other writings. Chapter four is a summary of the *Living Flame*, much shorter than the original but faithful to content and dynamic. Chapters five to eight deal with each of the four stanzas of the poem—their teachings, insights, and key themes. Finally, the conclusion focuses on six suggestions for readers as they approach this wonderful book.

CHAPTER ONE
JOHN'S VISION OF LOVE

The *Living Flame of Love* is the final chapter in John's vision of love. It describes the end of a journey that began in longings of love that became an experience of purification for the person seeking union. The person in his or her journey then passed through a period of illumination regarding the God of love and his or her own need of love. Then the person reached the early stage of union in spiritual betrothal. *The Living Flame of Love* picks up from the final stage of union in the love of spiritual marriage and describes, in great beauty, several aspects of this final stage in the union of love. All these ideas are part of John's wonderful vision of love.

John of the Cross is the doctor of divine and human love. Love fills his personal life and his entire system. His Trinitarian theology, his vision of humanity, his understanding of creation, his spirituality, and his ascetical program all focus on love. His vision of love is not some emotionally comforting approach to life. He saw and experienced this world at its worst and still proclaimed a call to universal love. Many writers have emphasized the spiritual value of a life of love, but John's vision is more expansive and integrated than approaches presented by anyone else. He begins with the inner life of the Trinity as a life of mutual love, and this becomes the model for everything else. He also sees the world as a gift of God's love, attracting us to appreciate how much God loves us. He is convinced that God has placed all around us innumerable invitations to return this love. Those who seek union with God in love must respond in love by undertaking a journey of love, motivated by love, sustained by love, transformed by love, in order to find union in love. God can only love the divine self, nothing else and no one else can satisfy the perfection of God. For men and women who are willing to make this journey of love the Holy Spirit of love transforms them to such an extent that they share in the divine life by total participation, becoming God while still retaining their own individuality (see C. 32.6). Thus, God recognizes them as the divine self and loves them as God loves self. John sees everything about humanity as part of God's project of love, and everything that happens to us as being integral to God's strategy of love.

God of love

John's understanding of God is the point of departure for his life and his ministry of spiritual direction and writing. His understanding of God's inner life and of God's strategy of love in salvation history is best expressed in John's nine "Romances." These beautiful poems serve as the point of departure for John's vision of life and act as a prologue to all his major works. Described by one author as "the Gospel of John of the Cross,"[1] these nine poems present the inner life of the Trinity as a life of love that overflows in creation, the

Incarnation, Redemption, and the history of salvation. John sees this shared love in the intercommunication of the Trinity as foundational for disciples' return journey to God.

John's mystical vision of God's strategy of love begins in the first "Romance" with the inner life of God, which is one love that unites them. There are three persons, but "One love in them all makes them one Lover." "For the three have one love," John writes. The three persons are together in constant unifying love. The Father then expresses how he loves the Son and how he could extend that love to others who are like the Son and love the Son. The Father offers the Son a bride (the created world) who will love him, and the Son says he will only choose a bride who "will burn with your (the Father's) love."

So the purpose of creation is to extend the love between Father and Son. The Father tells the Son to let creation begin, "For your love has deserved it," and the Son says he will give creation his love and lift up creation's love in return to the Father. The Son's love becomes so great that he is incarnated, "the lover becomes like the one loved." In his new life he affirms his love is so strong "I will die for her" and "I will restore her to you." So the cycle of love returns to the Trinity from which it started. John of the Cross confirms the essential conviction of God's own inner life of love and of our challenge to live and spread that love.[2] John understands that the boundless love that unites the Trinity, that immense love that proceeds and unifies the Persons, overflows to the world which is seen as the bride of the Son. The Father's love for the Son leads to the Son's spiritual marriage with the world. The Son so loves the world that in the Incarnation he becomes like the one he loves. He redeems the world and then takes the world, tenderly in his arms, and raises it up to the Father as a return of love. Thus, God's strategy of love runs full circle.

God's love draws us to divine love. This vision of God as essentially love that reaches out in love to the world and to each of us to embrace us all in divine love is the point of departure for understanding John's work. This divine love transforms our human love into an extension, and then a participation, in God's own life of love. It permeates all John's poems and commentaries, as they take us step by step along the journey of love. It reaches its most profound expression in the *Living Flame of Love* when the Holy Spirit absorbs the person into this immense love of God. John tells us not to be surprised at God's wonderful gifts, but at times we ignore this suggestion and we protect ourselves by believing in an unreal, remote God.

In a world where so many struggle to grasp the meaning of life, the understanding of God, the mystery of evil, sin, and the horrors of a world steeped in selfishness, hatred, and oppression, this vision of a world purified and transformed by the Living Flame of Love offers us a context in which to live, a calling to which we can respond, and a hope that will satisfy all our yearnings.

A world of love

In John's vision, the created world surrounds us with God's love. In the "Romances" the Father gives the world to the Son as a bride, and the Son transforms the world and re-gives it to the Father. Creation is a gesture of love between Father and Son that is then extended to men and women who have eyes to see the wonders of God. In John's writings there is no sign of "flight from the world," as seen in so much piety. While John opposes attachment to anything other than God and any movement towards absolutizing one's desire for creatures instead of God, he loved the beauty of the world with a refinement never found in men and women who lack spiritual vision. "If you purify your soul of attachments and desires, you will understand things spiritually. If you deny your appetite for them, you will enjoy their truth, understanding what is certain in them" (S. 49). John views the world through a different lens than we often do, and so everything changes for him. Love made John see everything in a new way, in a real way. At the same time he realizes that everything around him is a gift of love, and all the world speaks of the presence of a loving God. John tells us that this revelation of God "produces a symphony of love in the world." It is like "a supper that refreshes and deepens love" (C. 14-15.27).

In the early part of the spiritual journey creatures are insufficient means to lead to God, and one must detach oneself from everything. However, in the ascetical phase of the journey the consideration of creatures helps us appreciate the greatness of God's love and generosity in creation. This awakens our love for God. "Only the hand of God, her Beloved, was able to create this diversity and grandeur" (C. 4.3). When we look at the world around us, we can see traces of God's presence in creatures, and like the bride in the *Spiritual Canticle* we become "anxious to see the invisible beauty that caused this visible beauty" (C. 6.1). So, as we journey to God's love we learn to appreciate how God has lovingly transformed the whole world so that it now reveals the divine presence. Speaking of every aspect of the world, John says that God "having looked at them, with his image alone, clothed them in beauty" (C. 5). John includes the whole cosmos in his loving appreciation: "woods" are the basic elements of the universe, "thickets" refer to the teaming of animals, "green meadows" are the stars and planets, and "flowers" are angels and saintly individuals (C. stanza 4). As one journeys onward, "the soul becomes aware of Wisdom's wonderful harmony and sequence in the variety of her creatures and works" (C. 14-15.25).

At times this harmony of a world of love is shattered, and we see the destruction of the concept of love. There are so many people whose lives are filled with violence, untruthfulness, fear, hate, and oppression. Humanity has created its own hell on earth by driving love out of our lives. People around us, sometimes friends, and often ourselves, make unloving decisions that destroy us from within. We evidence a lot of conscious and unconscious resistance to God's love and illumination. However, even when love is lacking, we always retain remembrance of the call to love that is integral to our personalities. Sometimes we see love and it motivates us to appreciate our call; at other times our world cries out for love, and that too can motivate us to respond. God's love—our hope—overwhelms and overcomes the depressing misery of our world.

While aware of life's problems, we must maintain a mature focus on love. John's vision of love includes this conviction that we are surrounded by God's love. He abandons former spiritualities' negative approach to the world and focuses our attention on a renewed world. He challenges us to see the world differently than previously, to appreciate its beauty and wonder, and to realize all this is the result of God's love. At first the world is a sign of God's love and we get to know God through creatures. While at first creation is a reflection of God's love, it later becomes identified with God—"My Beloved is the mountains, the lonely wooded valleys, strange islands, and resounding rivers " (C. 14). In the *Living Flame* John changes the focus, suggesting that we get to know the created world through God and not God through creatures (F.4. 5). This is an awakening to a vision of God's love in creation. The world calls us to God and challenges us to appreciate the hidden presence of divine love that surrounds us.

Invitations of love

We were created for love and will be constantly unfulfilled until we are filled with love which is the ultimate reason for everything we do and are (C. 29.3). The human heart seeks meaning and fulfillment and finds them in love. *God surrounds men and women with all kinds of invitations to love.* Each of us finds that we are restless until we give ourselves to a life of love. So, God places the first invitation to love deep within our own hearts. If we do not answer this invitation to love we will never be the people we were created to be. We know God because of the love God gives to us.

Creation all around us reminds us of God's abundant love, for God has poured out a thousand graces and clothed the world with reflections of divine love. Throughout the spiritual life *creation provides invitations to love.* Reflecting on the wonders of creation we appreciate how it teaches us so much about life, beauty, seasons, rhythms, interdependence, and healthfulness. Creation is one of God's great invitations to love. It points us to the greatness, excellence, and generosity of God. "[O]nly the hand of God, her Beloved, was able to create this diversity and grandeur" (C. 4.3). In looking at creation one inevitably appreciates the awesomeness of God and God's overwhelming love for us. John also insists that we include men and women in appreciating God's love in creation: "Oh, then, soul, most beautiful among all creatures" (C. 1.7).

A further way in which *God invites a person to love is by means of the intense and unfulfilled longings* that he or she experiences. A person feels the pain of God's absence and longs for God's healing and delightful presence (C. 9.3). When John describes the profound desire of a person for the love of God he is speaking about something at the core of our humanity—an existential yearning to be who we are called to be. This desire can only be satisfied when the person "could plunge into the unfathomable spring of love" (C. 12.9). This desire is lovesickness that has no remedy except in the pursuit of love, for "love is incurable except by things in accord with love" (C. 11.1). "The reason for this is that love of God is the soul's health, and the soul does not have full health until love is complete" (C. 11.11). Eventually, everything that is not the pursuit of love wearies a person. God has made us in such a way that we have within us the invitation to seek love, for it is only love that can bring fulfillment in life.

God draws us to love by effecting within us a distaste for all things other than God and by a self-forgetfulness achieved by the love of God (C. 1.20). John calls these actions of God in the depth of a person "touches" or "wounds of love." This infused love creates a passion of love and draws the person to God. By these means God draws a person, raises him or her up, detaches from creatures, and attaches him or her to divine life. Thus, God enkindles the will and draws the understanding. These powerful invitations to love leave a person feeling that God has stolen his or her heart through love (C. 9.4). The whole spiritual journey consists essentially in God drawing a person to union through constant invitations to love, for "the soul drinks of the beloved's very own love that he infuses in her" (C. 26.7). God in dealing with an individual makes use of nothing other than love, draws him or her to love in everything, until the person knows how to do nothing else than love and walk always with the Bridegroom in the delights of love (C. 27.8). By drawing the person and infusing him or her with love God makes one worthy and capable of that love (C. 32.5).

Once the stage of beginners has passed God leads us into the depths of divine love (C. Prologue.3). *God invites us to love by teaching and leading us to love.* First God awakens love in our hearts passively in contemplation and when we respond God places his grace and love in us. Throughout the journey God shows the person how to love God as perfectly as possible, "teaching her to love purely, freely, and disinterestedly, as he loves us, God makes her love him with the very strength with which he loves her" (C. 38.4).

At this point *a person also sees an invitation of God in the many gifts he or she has received.* Aware of God's awesome generosity, he or she feels drawn to respond. This is equally true when one sees how generous God is to others too. They and their gifts are traces of God's presence that fills one with love. A person can follow these footprints that lead to God (C. 25.2-3).

One of the extraordinary ways in which *God constantly invites us to union in love is by the divine presence within us.* God is present to us by essence, by grace, and by spiritual affection. Reflecting on these ways of God being present, "the soul feels an immense hidden being from which God communicates to her some semi-clear glimpses of his divine beauty" (C. 11.4). These lead the person to ardently long for what is hidden in this presence.

Responses of love

One of the simplest ways of understanding John's challenges to those who seek union with God in love is to say they are called to *make choice-oriented decisions of love* at every point in life. These are not the many minor decisions of every day but are significant decisions or choices that are always motivated by love. These decisions imply sacrifice—what up to that time one may have valued must now be renounced for something better, in this case life with God. In responding to the call to spiritual growth a person makes a series of choices for a totally new direction in life—for a life based on love. These decisions change a person. Centering one's whole life on love only makes sense when one chooses it, lives it, and becomes enthralled by it.

The person who is united with God in the union of love must *abandon interest in creatures and seek God in faith and love.* This is a painful experience, and "love seems unbearably rigorous with the soul" (C. 1.18). But this self-denial is a sign of a person who truly loves God and has chosen to trust in God's love and friendship. Having purified all false loves the person is dried out and ready to be set on fire. At this time, the person "lives by dying until love, in killing her, makes her live the life of love, transforming her in love" (C. 7. 4). Love motivates a person to persevere in love in spite of the sufferings.

In his book on the *Dark Night*, John offers a program for a person's response in love. He calls it "the science of love," and offers readers *ten steps in the journey to God.* This is "an infused loving knowledge that both illumines and enamors the soul, elevating it step by step to God, its creator. For it is only love that unites and joins the soul to God" (N.2. 18.5).[3] The person centers his or her life on God and with impatient love cannot rest. Rather, he or she endures no delays in the on-going pursuit of God, has no further interest in self but only on pleasing God in everything. Anything that is not centered on love one finds distracting and wearisome. Such a person becomes impatient and bold in the pursuit of love.

The person now has no other work than to love, and neither desires nor hopes for any reward other than growth in love. *He or she realizes that only an ongoing response of love brings health,* for the love of God is the soul's health. "In the measure that love increases she will be healthier, and when love is perfect she will have full health" (C. 11.11). So, the person employs all his or her faculties and possessions in loving response to God.

A further response is to savor the effects of God's love within us. These touches or wounds of love are responses to God's gifts of love or painful reactions to unfulfilled love. These experiences can be painful but also refresh and renew.

The Living Flame of Love 13

Those who truly love God strive never to fail in this love, and their constant exercise of love leads to growth in virtue. At this time the Holy Spirit further awakens love in a person and accompanies him or her on the journey to reach God.

"[T]rue and perfect love knows not how to keep anything hidden from the beloved" (C. 23.1). At this point *one totally surrenders to love*. Surrender means giving up something we previously cherished and it also means giving oneself over to a new and overwhelmingly attractive cause. "Everything I do I do with love, and everything I suffer I suffer with the delight of love" (C. 28.8). This surrender to love is important for "there is no greater or more necessary work than love" (C. 29.1). So, one's complete self-gift to God corresponds to God's complete self-gift to the individual. There is no other priority; all else is very secondary. So, the person withdraws into solitude.

With the union of spiritual marriage, *a person "desires to employ herself in those things proper to love"* (C. 36.3). This includes receiving the joy and savor of love, desiring to become like the Beloved, rejoicing in the communications of knowledge of love. This "overflows into the effective and actual practice of love" (C. 36.4). A person now focuses exclusively on the object of his or her love and gives self totally to that love.

A journey of love

When we speak of God we need to speak of the ways we encounter God, for we find and know God in our experience of search. In the *Living Flame* John tells us more about the end of our journey than do most other spiritual writers. However, he also emphasizes the journey, especially in his other three major works: the *Ascent of Mount Carmel*, the *Dark Night of the Soul*, and the *Spiritual Canticle*. John presents two aspects of our journey; two parallel and complementary ways to God that are both necessary. He emphasizes the journey of faith in the *Ascent* and *Dark Night*, where he uses the symbolism of the dark night. He concentrates on the journey of love in the *Spiritual Canticle* and the *Living Flame*, where he uses matrimonial symbolism. Commenting on truths that are infused into a person through faith, he says, "Over this sketch of faith the sketch of love is drawn in the will of the lover" (C. 12.7). So, these two plans of God are imprinted on one's inner spirit, and both are necessary. In fact, the journey of faith is insufficient, unless it ends in confident, loving self-gift. John insists that the purpose of the *Dark Night* is to describe "a soul's conduct along the spiritual road that leads to the perfect union with God through love" (N. Title). While many seekers run to John for his way of faith in darkness, we need to remember that his way of love is more important. Speaking about the dark and glad night and the dense darkness it brings, John adds, ". . . love alone, which at this period burns by soliciting the heart for the Beloved, is what guides and moves her, and makes her soar to God" (N.2. 25.4). Even in the midst of darkness a person feels loving affliction, companionship, and interior strength. John further adds that in these difficult times the person feels the dark fire of love, and the strength and warmth of love (N.2. 11.7).

A person who undertakes this journey through the nights is "fired by love's urgent longings," and travels "with no other light or guide than the one that burned in my heart" (N. stanzas 1, 3). The journey of love implies total commitment until one arrives at union and possession. It is a journey in which God is the primary Lover who teaches us a new way of loving. It is a journey in which love matures gradually. There are three steps in this journey. First, a person experiences a love of absence, or a presence in absence. When God is absent the person experiences divine transcendence. Second, there is the love of union, when in union one feels God in everything. Here one experiences love and goodness and true knowledge in participation of divine life. Third, there is the experience of union-absence. In union a person sees his or her own insufficiencies, feels anxiety, and although in union feels to be more distant than ever. These steps are God's way of training a person to love in a different way. God values strong love, and this journey is a process of love and self-surrender. "[T]his is why he loved her so much; he saw that her love was strong. . . alone and without other loves" (C. 31.5).

This looks like a journey we are making to find union with God, but it is a journey we are making together with God. Our part in this journey begins with the realization of our call to pursue a life of love, and we must deliberately reflect on this awesome reality. John's concern is that we attain unity in our affective lives and avoid all dispersion of love (A.1. 10.1). We have a personal calling to union with God in love. This demands that in this journey we can spend time alone in contemplative reflection, confront our perceived limitations and our willingness to be too easily content with a half-hearted calling. We need to think about our spiritual calling in a totally different way, appreciating that ultimately, spiritual growth is what God is doing in us, and so we will need to appreciate the sense of mystery of our life and surrender to this calling. Above all we must never give in to a reduced ideal of our calling. We must be totally committed to the pursuit of love.

This response to love has two parts. It is a journey away from everything that is not God. "[T]he soul claims here that in order not to fail God she failed all that is not God, that is herself and all other creatures, losing all these for love of him" (C. 29.10; also C. 26.2). Then the journey is towards God along the path John indicates. In the journey, a person will keep watch over his or her heart, seek God through painful darkness, and yearn for the healing illumination of love. In suffering for love a person will find himself or herself transformed in a new kind of life where every act is love until he or she learns God's ways of loving.[4]

The Living Flame of Love

Those who wish to journey to union with God in love are assisted in their journey by the Living Flame of Love. The Living Flame, who is none other than the Holy Spirit, accompanies each one at every stage of the journey. In the early stages, when one enters contemplation, the Living Flame purifies the person's imperfections in order to prepare him or her for the inflow of God's love and for the transformation that will come later. At this time the Living Flame afflicts the person and allows him or her to feel dryness, darkness, distress, and lack of self-knowledge. It is a time of trials for the intellect, memory, and will. The Flame is oppressive in its purifying, and later in its illuminating actions within a person.

The Living Flame is a fire that consumes, transforms, and enflames a person, a permanent presence that takes over all actions, making them conform to God's ways. Thus, the Living Flame transforms the person in one's deepest center, motivating him or her to move to God in deeper love. The Holy Spirit burns within the soul, purifies its former failings, enlarges its experience, and leads it to healthfulness. In this spiritual journey the Living Flame moves a person away from satisfaction in creatures, transforms the spiritual faculties so that they focus on God, and leads the person to find satisfaction in God alone.

The *Living Flame of Love* brings full circle John's vision of love, which is also God's strategy of love. Having started with the vision of the Trinity's mutual love, we now end with the seeker's participation and absorption in the life of God. The Holy Spirit has taught, led, guided, and transformed a person into divine love. The Flame "makes the soul live in God spiritually and experience the life of God. . . the spirit and the senses, transformed in God, enjoy Him in a living way, which is to taste the living God—that is, God's life, eternal life" (F. 1.6). Having drawn a person through purification and illumination, and thrilled him or her with spiritual betrothal, the Holy Spirit satisfied each one's longings for deeper love in spiritual marriage. The Living Flame brings about the person's union and transformation and reveals the divine life of love to each one, granting the capacity to vitally know and enjoy all the qualities of God, each one permeated by love. God and the individual mutually surrender in love, and the person is absorbed in the Trinity's inner life of love. In this final awakening of love a person, captivated and aroused in love, discovers God's cosmic vision of love and his or her own place within it.

CHAPTER TWO

PREPARATORY STAGES IN THE SPIRITUAL LIFE

In his other writings John indicates his conviction that there is a process through which a person passes on his or her journey to union with God. He sees the spiritual life as an unwavering search for a union in which a person not only finds God but also his or her true self. John tells us that God wants people to undertake this journey. "God gives many souls the talent and grace for advancing, and should they desire to make the effort they would arrive at this high state" (A. Prologue.3). This journey begins after a person "has been resolutely converted to his service" (N.1. 1.2). Once we start this journey, "the attainment of our goal demands that we never stop on this road" (A.1. 11.6). This journey is one of continual growth or regression, but never stationary, as the person passes through a series of stages. These stages correspond somewhat to the traditional divisions of the spiritual life—the beginners' stage of purification, the proficients' stage of illumination, and the stage of the perfect in union. John modified the approach by giving greater emphasis to the two transitions from purgation to illumination and from illumination to union. He called the transitions "nights".

These stages make up the journey to union with God in love. In the *Ascent of Mount Carmel* and the *Dark Night of the Soul* John focuses on this journey more from the perspective of faith, and in the *Spiritual Canticle* more from the perspective of love. So the journey is at once a journey of faith and love. There are fundamentally three steps: purification, illumination, and union, corresponding to the three phases of beginners, proficients, and perfect. There are also two very important transitions; the first marks the beginning of contemplation, and the second marks the total self-gift to the life of the Spirit. These stages are equally present whether one makes this journey as a journey of faith or as a journey of love. From the perspective of the journey of faith, the five stages are as follows:

1. A period of preparation and purification (active night of sense; A.1.)
2. The beginning of contemplation (passive night of sense together with some aspects of the active night of spirit; N.1.; A.2-3.)
3. Period of illumination (continuing passive night of sense and active night of spirit)
4. Major transition of life—total self-gift to the life of the Spirit (passive night of spirit; N.2.)
5. Stage of the perfect in union

From the perspective of the journey of love, the five stages are as follows:

1. A period of preparation (painful longings of love and ascetical practices; C.1-5)
2. The beginning of contemplation (illumination and intense personal longing; C.6-12)
3. Period of illumination continues

4. Betrothal and further intense painful longings (encounter, joy, and preoccupation; C. 13-21)
5. Stage of perfect (spiritual marriage, total union and fruits of union; C.22-35),
   Desire of union in glory (C.36-40). This final stage is also described in the *Living Flame of Love*.

When John writes the *Living Flame of Love* these stages are complete, and the person is already in the final stage of spiritual matrimony. However, in three digressions that John makes in commenting on the first three stanzas the person looks back over the journey that led to the present union. It was a painful journey, but it was a necessary preparation and well worth the sacrifices one had to make. Looking back it was less an effort-filled journey and more a learning experience of how to let go of false values and let God do all the work of drawing the person to divine life.

Looking back

The *Living Flame* deals with four aspects of the union achieved in spiritual marriage. As a person looks back on the earlier stages of the spiritual life he or she feels that the present delightful experience of spiritual marriage described in this poem is a reward for the many trials he or she has endured in reaching this state. Ordinarily, no one reaches this state of delight without having passed through many tribulations and trials. In the poem these are now ended, for the person is purified and suffers no more. John points out that these trials include temptations from the world, afflictions on the senses, and trials in the spirit. These purify a person in his or her sensory and spiritual parts and are a necessary preparation for union. A person must be purified, strengthened, refined in sense and spirit for shorter or longer periods, as God sees fit and according to the degree of union to which God wishes to raise him or her.

John seems to take whatever opportunity offers to digress to his favorite topic of the nights as preparations for the encounter with the Living Flame. He presents three principal digressions, and each one serves as an excursus on preparations for union. These digressions may seem to break or interrupt the unity and thematic development of the *Living Flame*, but they are very helpful for a person who wishes to make this journey to union. Here, we see John as theologian, teacher, and spiritual director, summarizing his previous teachings and even adding to them. The three digressions (some writers speak of four) form just over a third of the *Living Flame*. The first digression (F. 1.18-26) is a dramatic description of suffering in darkness. While John never uses the word "night" nor does he distinguish the two stages of the nights, nevertheless this digression is similar to book two of the *Dark Night*. The second digression (F. 2.23-31) addresses the purification of the spirit as a proof of fidelity. This is a time when God is reforming the person through the purification of the Flame. This is a different perspective than those found in the *Ascent* and *Dark Night*. The third digression (F. 3.18-67) is the largest and most detailed and is very similar to the teachings of the second book of the *Ascent*. It focuses on the purification of the three spiritual faculties of intellect, memory, and will. Some writers divide this third digression into two: a first part on the three spiritual faculties (F. 3.18-26) and a second part on spiritual direction and the three blind guides (F. 3.27-67). Moreover, some commentators add the line "Once obscure and blind" (F. 3.70-75) as part of the third digression.

It seems reflection on these past trials increases the person's sense of joy in the new life of the Living Flame. Through these trials and suffering described in the digressions a person acquires virtues, strength, and perfection, as God purifies and strengthens him or her for union in love. Few people reach the high state described in this poem because God finds few who are willing to endure the purification. God gives little tests, finds that many cannot endure even these, and so proceeds no further. Many want to advance, pray to do so, but are unwilling to be guided in the suffering that leads to the advancement they seek. Likewise, many long to walk in security and consolation but cannot accept the purification. So, the fire of love that unites and transforms in this poem, previously purified a person leading him or her through stages of purgation, illumination, and espousal. All these are preparatory for a person's advance to spiritual marriage which is described in this poem.

The purgative stage of beginners

John's writings begin when one enters the next phase after that of beginners, but he does say a lot about this phase of beginners in parentheses, asides, and digressions throughout his writings, especially when he looks back to former times. It is a time of struggle to overcome the attachments to satisfactions of sense, initial fervor, and meditation. Beginners evidence numerous imperfections that John categorizes under the seven deadly sins (N. 1). They want themselves more than they want God and often block God out of their lives. In the *Spiritual Canticle* John presents the individual as enthusiastically accepting the painful purification of this stage as a preparation for future union, and the pain takes on the characteristic of unfulfilled longings for love. This is a time of denial, sorrow, abandonment, spiritual dryness, and emptiness. John's focus is not annihilation but redirection, re-education, and preparation for transformation. For John, negation is not an end; it is part of the process of spiritual empowerment. It leads to liberating oneself from self-centered gratification and to the freedom to choose what is good. Above all, this is a time when a person strives to leave aside everything that does not lead to God. In his digressions in the *Living Flame* John has the following to say about the purgative stage of beginners.

The first stage of the spiritual life is the stage of purgation—the period of beginners. It is a discipline one must impose on oneself—a willingness to move away from self and everything that does not lead to life with God. "[P]ersons who truly love God . . . are content with nothing less than God" (C. 1.14). Rather, they maintain their spirit centered on God, persevere in prayer, and keep their hearts entirely set on God (C. 1.13). John of the Cross refers to this stage especially in the *Ascent* and also in the *Spiritual Canticle*. In these experiences of the "purgative way" a person feels oppressed, as he or she suffers deprivations and afflictions of spirit. At this time the flame of love is not gentle but afflictive. A person feels dryness, experiences darkness, suffers with self-knowledge, and feels wretched and distressed. This is a time of trials in the intellect, dryness in the will, and burdensome knowledge in the memory. Oppressed by the purifying flame, one finds no relief or consolation, rather oppression and abandonment. These sufferings are intense, but this is the only way to purify a person of all his or her weaknesses and to show the profound need of transformation. So, the Living Flame makes a person see and feel his or her own weaknesses. "It should be recalled that when the soul was in the state of spiritual purgation, which was at the time of the beginning of contemplation, this flame of God was not so friendly and gentle toward it" (F.1.18). It seems there is a war going on between the virtues and goodness of God and the negative habits of the individual. The brightness of the flame throws light on the darkest regions of one's inner spirit, causing confusion and pain to the soul. In this purgative way, "a person suffers great deprivation and feels heavy afflictions in his spirit, which ordinarily overflows into the senses, for this flame is extremely oppressive" (F. 1.19).

Only those who have served God, shown great patience and constancy, and have endured the trials God sends, can advance along this road of denial, purification, and the cross. This is how God acts towards those ready to be led to union. It is a journey of many purgations, each related to a further degree of love. A person should never flee from these trials but face them with patience and constancy. These trials will be exterior and interior, spiritual and bodily, great and small. This is the way to combat evil habits, and it will deaden evil, purify and strengthen the person. People should rejoice in being chosen for this, for undergoing these trials is the way to a higher state.

The illuminative stage of proficients

Purgation is painful, but so too is illumination, as God gradually communicates knowledge of divine life to a person. This takes place in contemplation, an experience in which the person is passive, as God becomes his or her teacher and guide. In other words the previous active night of sense gives way to the passive night of sense, as a person willingly surrenders to God's purifying activity in prayer. He or she lets go of all false images of God, and God communicates a more perfect image of divine life. At this time a person can no longer meditate, nor does he or she desire to apply the imagination. Rather, the person finds satisfaction in remaining in a loving attention towards God. In his digressions, John has a lot to say about this period.

The purifying flame illuminates a person

At this time the illuminating flame enables the eye of the soul to see what previously it could not. Although the flame is essentially loving, at this time it seems oppressive. The person's inner spirit is hard, dry, and unfeeling—totally unprepared for loving union until the darkness, hardness, dryness, and lack of feeling for spiritual values are driven out. The flame overwhelms the person, enlarges, widens, and makes him or her capable of receiving love. The person experiences the flame's transforming actions as oppressive, unpleasant, and bitter, and sees nothing except his or her own weaknesses, misery, poverty, and evil. However, God transforms the person, softens, pacifies, and clarifies him or her, preparing for the union that lies ahead. God allows this purification in varying degrees and intensity, according to the divine will for each one. It is a preparation for transformation.

As God leads a person to focus on spiritual things the appetite is torn away from sensual things and things of the world. Once a person becomes accustomed to spiritual things and endowed with fortitude and constancy, God weans him or her away from earlier focuses and places him or her in the state of contemplation. This happens when a person finds it hard to meditate and finds no further satisfaction in it but only dryness. At this time God becomes the agent and the person the receiver. God works in the person who remains passive and in contemplation grants a loving knowledge.

At this point when a person has lost the satisfaction found in meditation, he or she should not even seek such satisfaction. Rather, one should passively remain in God with a loving attention. God and the individual commune through simple loving knowledge and attention. To achieve this approach a person must purify natural operations and become quiet, peaceful, serene, detached from satisfactions—sensory or spiritual. When one is conscious of being placed in this solitude and spiritual listening, the person should even lay aside the active components of the practice of loving attention to be available for whatever God desires. He or she should only return to the practice of loving attention when no longer experiencing the inner idleness of spiritual listening. A person can recognize this change when he or she feels a certain peace, calm, and inward passive absorption. Once drawn to contemplation a person should no longer meditate, nor seek spiritual satisfactions, but remain detached from everything in order to receive God's communications passively. Then contemplation gives light for the understanding and love for the will. The individual is often unaware of what is happening but feels a sense of withdrawal and estrangement from all creatures and an inclination towards solitude in the love and life of the spirit. These blessings are inestimable, hidden anointings of the Holy Spirit, secretly filling the person with spiritual gifts. A person must not disturb these gifts by even the least act of memory, intellect, or will, or by any act of his or her own. This is a time to passively receive.

During the journey one should avoid three blind guides

A person must not be influenced by blind guides. There are three blind guides who can lead a person astray: the spiritual director, the devil, and oneself. The harm done by a spiritual guide interfering in this period of blessing can be immense. It might not be seen immediately but in the long term it is ruinous. In this beginning of contemplation God blesses the person with loving knowledge that is serene, peaceful, and solitary, and he or she withdraws from the senses, leaves aside meditation, and all sense satisfaction. In contemplation the activity of the senses and discursive meditation end, and God now becomes the sole agent who leads the solitary and silent individual. Once the person has reached quiet recollection in which the functioning of the faculties cease, it is not only useless to repeat the process to attain recollection it would also be harmful and a great distraction. Now, the Holy Spirit is the person's principal guide. At this time a person is not doing anything, but God is, drawing the person to complete detachment of sense and spirit and to emptiness, so that he or she can be ready for the silent and secret communications of God. A person becomes ready for God's communications in nakedness and emptiness of sense and spirit, in order to purify natural operations and affections which cannot lead to God but only impede the process.

The second blind guide capable of thwarting a person's recollection is the devil. When a person has withdrawn from creatures and receives the anointing of the Holy Spirit the devil is filled with sadness and envy, and strives to intrude in this withdrawal by making the person revert to the work of the senses. He distracts him or her, drawing such a one out of solitude and recollection. Some people who do not understand the road they are travelling easily incline to sensible satisfactions and the knowledge provided by the devil, and thus lose the solitude God provides. For small satisfactions a person impedes God's work in solitude, thinking doing something is better than waiting in solitude for God's anointing. The devil with very little causes harm to a person alluring him or her away from solitude. Few people avoid this bait that the devil provides at the passage from sense to spirit as he deceives a person by feeding the sensory part with sensible things. At this point a person often fails to see the potential loss and thus also fails to enter sublime recollection. If the devil fails in his effort, he strives to make the person revert to sense by horrors, fears, bodily pains, noise—anything to draw him or her away from the interior spirit. Unfortunately, the devil finds blocking the person's enrichment in solitude easy, and he accomplishes it with little effort. People drawn to God in solitude and recollection should withdraw from all labors of the senses. Formerly this may have helped, now it is an obstacle. God is now the primary agent, and a person needs to live in detachment and freedom of spirit so as not to impede its peace and tranquility.

The third blind guide is oneself by not understanding what is happening. Since such a person is accustomed to acting by means of the senses and discursive recollection, one now thinks he or she is doing nothing when God introduces him or her into emptiness and solitude. When in the idleness of spiritual peace, a person feels empty and filled with dryness and displeasure. God wants the person in silent quietude but the person desires to act through his or her own efforts with the intellect and imagination. One should note even though one does not seem to be making progress in this quiet solitude one is advancing well. Although a person is doing nothing with his or her faculties, God is achieving a lot, even though the person does not realize it. So, one should abandon oneself to God, and God as the primary guide will assure advancement.

The first unitive stage— spiritual espousal

This is a time when a person gives himself or herself totally to God. This is a critical moment in the spiritual life when God prepares a person for special communications. It is also a time of painful ongoing purification, for the person still longs for deeper union in the spiritual marriage that lies ahead. It is a time for the total transformation of the spiritual faculties of intellect, memory, and will. God becomes so important to the seeker that all else seems a waste of time.

John deals with this especially in his third digression. We know how a person's faculties of memory, intellect, and will suffer when empty, and can appreciate how they rejoice when filled. When these caverns of the spiritual faculties are not emptied of every affection, they do not appreciate their own capacity. Without purification any little thing can burden and bewitch them. Yet until they are completely emptied they cannot be filled. When they are empty and pure, they feel intense pain at their own emptiness and yearn for what they lack, namely God. When the spiritual appetite is emptied of all affection for creatures and a person still lacks communication with God in union, then the pain of emptiness is intense, and becomes even worse when now and then one catches a glimpse of the union that lies ahead. The intellect thirsts for divine wisdom. The will hungers for the perfection of love. The memory seeks the possession of God. "The Blessed Trinity inhabits the soul by divinely illumining its intellect with the wisdom of the Son, delighting its will in the Holy Spirit, and by absorbing it powerfully and mightily in the delightful embrace of the Father's sweetness" (F. 1.15).

It is worth remembering that the flame of love which in this present poem is gentle and transforming in loving union is the same flame that was formerly oppressive, as it assailed a person in periods of purification. At this time the person accomplishes a lot when he or she learns how to do nothing, thereby becoming ready to advance. For example, if a person empties the intellect of knowledge, spiritual and natural, he or she becomes free to receive new knowledge from God. When the intellect is active it is withdrawing from God. The intellect must withdraw from its normal object of knowledge so as to journey to God in faith, for a person is united to God in faith and not in knowledge. When the intellect becomes empty it can advance by focusing itself in faith. At first this is darkness to the intellect. But the intellect cannot know God but must journey in submission in faith. This is contemplative knowledge which is dark to the intellect. Likewise, love is present in the will without specific objects or parts. God informs both intellect and will with knowledge and love. The will does not need to feel idle at this time. It does not need to make acts of love, for God takes over and fills it with divine love. As previously with the intellect, the will advances when it is empty of other loves. If the will does not go back to former loves, it advances, even though it does not experience God in a particular way. It enjoys God in the general infusion of divine love. In solitary quietude the person loves God above all else that is loveable. He or she makes progress only when he or she does not and cannot dwell on any other object of love. Such a person's will is now detached from its normal objects, so it can love or let God love in it. Similarly, the memory detaches itself from all forms and figures in the imagination for God cannot be possessed in this way. When completely empty the memory can be filled with the future of God.

God graces a person bringing him or her to solitude and emptiness regarding faculties and activities, for God wants to speak to people's hearts. Reigning in the person in calm and peace God takes the initiative and feeds the person without the activity of the senses. God values this passivity, tranquility, solitary sleep, and forgetfulness.

This desire for the vision of God contains no pain, since the person possesses God in desire. The more the person desires God, the more he or she possesses God, and this possession delights the individual. Thus, the greater a person's desires for God the greater the satisfaction and delight rather than pain and suffering. Possession of God can be through grace or through union (F. 3.24). The latter includes communication. The former is spiritual espousal, the latter spiritual marriage. The person's will and God's will are now one, and thus he or she attains possession of God by will and grace. This is not comparable to spiritual marriage. To attain this latter the person needs God to purify, beautify, and refine it so as to prepare it for union. During this time of espousal the preparations of the Holy Spirit become more sublime and the caverns of the faculties experience extreme and delicate longing for fullness. A person's desire for God is more refined and profound, as it prepares for the union of spiritual matrimony, a union that is not only affective but effective. This is the final stage in the spiritual life and the one that is presumed throughout the poem and commentary on the *Living Flame.*

We have seen that the *Living Flame of Love* is not itself developmental. John stated that he had spoken of "the highest degree of perfection one can reach in this life" in other poems he had written—referring primarily to the *Spiritual Canticle.* The stanzas of the *Living Flame* "treat of a love within this very state of transformation that has a deeper quality and is more perfect" (F. Prologue.3) However, in John's three digressions found in the first three stanzas, he looks back to the various stages of the spiritual life. These must be taken in the context of God's plan to help each person to love God more, and this call to love will always include purification. All these experiences led to this present stage of union where "with time and practice, love can receive added quality, . . . and become more intensified" (F. Prologue.3). These preparatory stages are presumed throughout the *Living Flame.*

Appendix One: Components of spiritual marriage

John insists that the *Living Flame* deals with four facets of the relationship of spiritual marriage. He describes spiritual marriage in stanzas 22-40 of the *Spiritual Canticle*. In spiritual marriage a person is at rest in the loving embrace of her Beloved. According to John, what are the characteristics of spiritual marriage?

Spiritual marriage is an experience of transformation that includes peaceful security, gratitude, communication of special knowledge, mutual surrender, equality in love, possession of the Lover, celebration, and total communion.

Transformation

In spiritual marriage the bride has reached a new level of existence in which all the spiritual faculties have been perfected by God, and all actions are now divine, for God acts in and through the soul. God has made all this possible. In this new state, which is a transformation in love, the bride finds abundance, fullness, security, peace and delight—more than at any other period in life (C. 22.5). This transformation is only found when there is a likeness of love and God's will and the person's are in complete conformity.

Peaceful security

All the negative effects of appetites have been controlled by the power of Christ's cross. The person is now secure in the transforming presence of God, and is aware of the constant protection of God. "When the soul has become established in the quietude of solitary love for her

Bridegroom. . . she is settled in God, and God in her. . . for now God is her guide and her light" (C. 35.1).

Gratitude

With humility the person appreciates the many gifts received from God, especially the effects of God's work of purification. Moreover, a person is also grateful for God's many gifts to others.

Communication of special knowledge

Spiritual marriage includes the revelation of special secrets. A person receives a deeper appreciation of divine mysteries, especially the Incarnation and Redemption. It is in solitude that God communicates special knowledge.

Mutual surrender

This begins in friendship and mutual gratitude, but deepens in spiritual marriage, and then in this mutual surrender to consuming love, God communicates mystical knowledge. In "such supreme and generous love" (C. 27.2), each surrenders self totally to the other and this union becomes a participation in divine life. "The union wrought between the two natures and the communication of the divine to the human in this state is such that even though neither changes its being both appear to be God" (C. 22.4).

Equality in love

The Bridegroom and bride are bound together in strong love, immersed in love (C. 31.5). A person discovers that love is the only focus of life. In the *Spiritual Canticle* the bride says: "All the ability of my soul and body. . . move in love and because of love. Everything I do I do with love, and everything I suffer I suffer with the delight of love" (C. 28.8). Everything is now done for love, and the bride searches "[T]o reach the consummation of the love of God. . . to love God as purely and perfectly as he loves her in order to repay him by such love. . . to love the Bridegroom as perfectly as he loves her" (C. 38.2).

Possession of the Lover

This is the fundamental experience of the person who feels embraced by God and experiences the full realization of union. All previous longings are now ended and this mutual possession is felt in the substance of the person's soul. The lovers' encounter in the wine cellar is the last and most intimate degree of love—the last of seven degrees of love corresponding to the seven gifts of the Holy Spirit (C. 26.3).

Celebration

The Bridegroom and bride celebrate each other. They celebrate the efforts, gifts, struggles, and virtues of their loving fidelity. The Bridegroom and bride enjoy together their love for each other and this brings refreshment, solace, and mutual rejoicing (C. 30.2). A person can also celebrate his or her own fortitude and perseverance. In this celebration a person re-finds all values in God. This vision of integration of life gives a real objective view of life.

Total communion

Spiritual marriage is an experience of unity in which the whole human nature is harmoniously integrated. This contemplative union includes a communion, mutual sharing, and appreciation of each other's gifts. The goal is not just union but a union that implies total renewal of self in which humanity is not destroyed but reaches its full potential. The seeker wants to be alone with her Lover, and he appreciates her growth in transforming solitude. The lovers long for the deeper union of eternity, nothing blocks this now except living in the body.

Appendix two: Some reflections on spiritual direction

John as spiritual director

In his third digression John comments at length on spiritual direction. Elsewhere in his works he also deals with this important topic. John of the Cross was an experienced spiritual director involved in the formation and personal guidance of friars and nuns from the earliest time of the reform, first in Mancera de Abajo, in Pastrana, as rector in Alcalá de Henares, and then as chaplain and confessor to the nuns of the monastery of the Incarnation in Avila. At times he was asked to look into special cases, such as that of the Augustinian nun, Maria de Olivares, or the investigation of the prayer life of a Carmelite nun—a copy of which we have in the minor works of John. Throughout his life, the ministry of spiritual direction was of paramount importance to John. In spite of his many responsibilities, he would prolong his guidance of others through his letters and through the maxims of light and love—those short sayings he often left in the places of the nuns and friars in their dining room. While John focused his attention especially on the nuns and friars of the reform, he also reached out to many clergy, religious and laity, for so many sought his guidance.[5] Of course his major works became sources of guidance for many of his directees, along with some of his minor works such as "The Precautions," "Counsels to a Religious," his letters, and in some of the "Maxims of Light and Love." John of the Cross' spiritual direction continues today to the innumerable followers who find guidance in his extraordinary writings.

Qualities needed in a spiritual director

John stresses the importance of spiritual direction. "The virtuous soul that is alone and without a master is like a lone burning coal; it will grow colder rather than hotter" (S. 7). At the outset of the *Ascent* he points out that some people do not enter the dark night because they are "without suitable and alert directors who will show them the way to the summit" (A. Prologue. 3). His worry is that these people then stay in their lowly methods of communion with God "because they receive no direction on breaking away from the methods of beginners" (A. Prologue. 3). In one of his letters to Juana de Pedraza, John stresses the importance of a spiritual director. "A soul should find its support wholly and entirely in its director, for not to do so would amount to no longer wanting a director. And when one director is sufficient and suitable, all the others are useless or a hindrance" (L. 11). John felt strongly that each one should have a spiritual director; otherwise a person wanders around in the dark. "The blind man who falls will not get up alone in his blindness, and if he does, he will take the wrong road" (S. 11). In another saying he affirmed, "Consider how much more can be accomplished by two together than by one alone" (S. 9).

John of the Cross gives the distinct impression of being very concerned about the quality and preparation of spiritual directors, and several times he suggests it is difficult to find an accomplished spiritual director. Moreover, he has more negative comments than positive ones about the directors he has seen. In the *Living Flame*, where John expresses his concerns about blind spiritual guides, he tells his readers that they must be very careful in the selection of a spiritual director. Moreover, some who can be helpful in earlier phases of the spiritual life are unqualified to guide others in the later stages. John tells his readers that they need to find someone who is learned and discreet, and experienced in the spiritual life. He states that the foundation for guiding a soul to life in the spirit is *knowledge* and *discretion*, but the director must also have *experience* of what a true and pure spirit is (F. 3. 30). These qualities are essential even before one undertakes spiritual direction, however, throughout the guidance of others the director must be a person given to *holiness* of life. In this context John constantly addresses the director's need of faith, hope, love, self-control, and commitment to prayer.

In addition to these foundational qualities, John tells directors that they must be able to *resist pressures* from their own directees, who seek guidance to their own liking (N.1. 2.3). John wants a director who will resist a directee's desire to do his or her own will (N.1 6.3). Along with this practical need the director should be able to *challenge* the pride of directees who focus on their own will and think the directors do not understand (N.1 2.3). So, the director should keep some *distance* from the directee and have less esteem for a directee's spirit and deeds, rather keeping him or her focused on humility in the journey.

The director's contributions begin with an *awareness that God is the primary guide.* "The soul, then, should avert that God is the principal agent in this matter, and that He acts as the blind man's guide who must lead it by the hand to the place it does not know how to reach" (F. 3.29). The work of the spiritual director is simply to facilitate this and not to get in the way of God's interventions in the life of the directee.

As mentioned already, John seeks a spiritual director who *understands the stages of the spiritual journey.* The spiritual director's task is to be a spiritual judge who gives pertinent instruction for each stage and requires full disclosure of spiritual life of the directee. In the early stages of the spiritual life the director should be able to recognize the signs of the purification of the soul in the dark night (A. Prologue 6). Problems can arise if the director does not, for sometimes the opposite happens and directors think someone is in the dark night when they are not. The important thing is to help the directee be ready for the challenges of God. "[T]he chief concern of spiritual directors with their penitents is the immediate mortification of every appetite" (A. 1. 12.6). Throughout the journey the director will need *humility* for in the dark night the directee finds no consolation in any teaching of the spiritual director (N.2 7.3), and the director must understand why. Moreover, he or she needs to realize that some souls cannot adequately explain to their director their experience of contemplation.

Problems associated with an incompetent spiritual director

John sees the potential for spiritual growth in many people, and tells us that God wants to draw as many as possible to undertake the spiritual journey to union in love. However, they are often *hindered by the absence or incompetence of spiritual directors*. In his prologue to the *Ascent* he states, "For some spiritual directors are likely to be a hindrance and harm rather than a help to these souls that journey on this road. Such directors have neither the enlightenment nor experience of these ways" (A.Prologue. 4). John goes on to say these directors are like the people who tried to build the tower of Babel and ended failures because they did not understand the language, and as a result nothing was accomplished.

John particularly stresses *the lack of judgment in spiritual directors*. Included in these wrong judgments would be that when someone is in darkness the director can suggest it is depression, or think that a person is falling back when they are without consolations! Then again the director often judges trials are the result of sin and makes suggestions of earlier practices of piety to correct them. "The director does not understand that now perhaps is not the time for such activity. Indeed, it is a period for leaving these people alone in the purgation God is working in them" (A. Prologue. 5). The problem of poor judgment seems to arise particularly at the transition to contemplation.

John also addresses *failures of directors in dealing with the spiritual visions* of directees, even saying that directors are often deluded in giving inappropriate importance to these visions. Thus, he comments on the lack of discretion in some directors in analyzing visions (A.2. 18.2). "[T]hese directors together with their penitents have gone astray and become bewildered" (A.2. 18.2). It is as if one blind man is guiding another blind man.

Some incompetent directors *burden their directees with their own neatly packaged methods.* They fail to guide along the way of humility. Moreover, they have the wrong attitude and give their directees poor instruction (A.2. 18.5). Thus, "the disciple is secretly fashioned after that of his spiritual father." The director gets too enthused by what he considers visions; he gets satisfaction from them as well as the directee.

Some do not understand the stages of the spiritual life and some especially do not appreciate the later stages. Often the spiritual director insists on active prayer when passivity and receptivity are needed. Directors need to be aware of their gifts and their own limitations; some are experts and others are general practitioners. The directee may not be able to make the whole journey with the same director. So, the directee needs to be free to change when he or she feels things are not right and the director no longer helpful.

The image of the spiritual director in the Living Flame

The directee should choose a spiritual director carefully. In his third digression which shows some similarities with the teaching of the *Ascent* on the purification of the spiritual faculties, John speaks at length about spiritual directors. He says that a person in this stage should avoid placing any obstacle in the way of the work of the Lord, pointing out that he or she "can cause this obstacle by allowing itself to be guided by another blind man" (F. 3.29). The first of the three blind men is the spiritual director! Because of his concern, John points out "it is very important that a person, desiring to advance in recollection and perfection, take care into whose hands he entrusts himself, for the disciple will become like the master" (F. 3.30). The problem for followers is that it is very hard to find an accomplished guide for the more sublime parts of the journey. If the director lacks the appropriate qualities he or she can cause great harm, especially by leading the soul back to earlier stages in the spiritual life when such a decision is totally inappropriate. John says such directors do not understand anything more than pertains to beginners and do not want the directee to pass beyond what the spiritual director can manage.

The director needs to be aware of the stages in spiritual development. Beginners focus on meditation, use their imagination, and find satisfaction in spiritual things, but God, as the primary agent, begins to move the person away from such devotion, and the director needs to know that he or she can no longer lead the directee as before but must lead away from meditation and any former desire for consolations. At this time the director needs to be aware that a person is being placed in a state of listening, loving attention, and readiness to follow the Lord's will. As the directee enters this state of contemplation, he or she emphasizes detachment from all sense satisfaction and receives profound blessings that neither the directee nor the director understand. Any interference by the spiritual director in these developments can cause great harm. "Although this damage is beyond anything imaginable, it is so common and frequent that scarcely any spiritual director will be found who does not cause it in souls God is beginning to recollect in this manner of contemplation" (F. 3.43). John describes such directors as blacksmiths who pound away at the faculties and lead the directee away from the silence and passivity in which God is working. The basic problem for these directors is that they do not understand the stages of prayer and the ways of the spirit, and cannot see that the directee is now ready for a new stage in spiritual growth. "God alone is the agent and one Who speaks secretly to the solitary and silent soul" (F. 3. 44). The director's interference is not only useless it is harmful. John claims the spiritual directors fail to understand the nature of recollection and spiritual solitude and impose activities of beginners.

The spiritual director must appreciate his or her role as God's assistant. John insists, "These directors should reflect that they themselves are not the chief agent, guide, and mover of souls in this matter, but that the principal guide is the Holy Spirit" (F. 3.46). The director is an instrument, facilitating God's guidance in directees. So, he or she should not impose his own methods on directees but lead them along the road God has chosen into solitude and freedom of spirit. John ends forcefully, "if he does not recognize it, he should leave them alone and not bother them" (F. 3. 46). In the seeming emptiness at this time God is purifying the three spiritual faculties. The trouble is that some directors do not understand contemplation because they have not reached it themselves, and so they hinder its development in others, turning them back to earlier practices in the spiritual life.

Some directors are ill-prepared and act recklessly. This intrusion in God's work in the directee is harmful. "These directors do not know what spirit is. They do a great injury to God and show disrespect toward Him by intruding with a rough hand where He is working" (F. 3. 54). "Perhaps in their zeal these directors err with good will because they do not know any better. Not for this reason, however, should they be excused for the counsels they give rashly, without first understanding the road and spirit a person may be following, and for rudely meddling in something they do not understand, instead of leaving the matter to one who does understand it" (F. 3.56). These directors who act recklessly will face punishment for not handling God's affairs with competence, or for vainly clinging to directees they are ill-prepared to help. Each director must know his or her limitations, not jealously hold on to directees with the abilities he or she has but let go and let the directee move to someone who knows more and can lead further. This implies giving directees freedom to move on and encouragement to do so, rather than possessively acting like a barrier, hindering the directee from advancement.

The directee today

Spiritual direction continues to be critically important for anyone pursuing the deeper development of spiritual life. Many good people give themselves to the ministry of spiritual direction and see themselves as guides or companions on the journey. While there are many excellent spiritual directors for the early stages of the spiritual life, there is still a lack of those who are qualified enough to lead people in the later stages of spiritual development. Many lack knowledge, discretion, and experience, and particularly fail to understand the stages in the development of the spiritual journey. John's concerns are equally present today. Many who long for a good spiritual director often fail to find one locally and must cope with guidance at a distance or through the internet. John of the

Cross can continue to guide others through his writings and the challenges and practical advice they present.

CHAPTER THREE
INTRODUCTION TO THE LIVING FLAME OF LOVE

Some preliminary comments

John of the Cross was the Discalced Carmelites' vicar provincial of Andalusia from October 1585 until April 1587. During that time, he resided in the monastery of Los Martires in Granada, on the lower slopes of the hill that led to the Alhambra palace.[6] This great southern city was for John as a writer what Toledo was for him as a poet. While living in Granada, John finished the *Spiritual Canticle* sometime in June of 1586 and gave a copy to Ana de Jesús, the superior of the convent in Granada. In the *Spiritual Canticle* John refers to "the explanation of the four stanzas that begin 'O Living Flame of Love'" (C. 31.7). So, the commentary (in this case the second redaction of the *Spiritual Canticle*) was already finished in 1586, meaning the commentary on the *Living*

Flame was probably written in the winter months of 1585-86. At the beginning of the *Living Flame*, John reminds Doña Ana de Peñalosa about his comments on spiritual marriage made in the *Spiritual Canticle* (F. Prologue.3).

John of the Cross was about 42 or 43 when he wrote this extraordinary masterpiece of spiritual insight. The poem was written only a short time before the commentary, both at the request of Doña Ana de Peñalosa. This period was one of intense obligations, work, and distractions, and John felt reluctant to write, especially the commentary. Nevertheless, he wrote the first redaction of the commentary in just fifteen days.

The "Living Flame" is the shortest of John's major poems—just twenty four lines in comparison to the forty lines of the "Dark Night," and two hundred in the final version of the "Spiritual Canticle." Although the poem is short, John seems on fire with his subject, and Fr. Gabriel calls the commentary "a book of fire."[7] While John's other works consider the spiritual journey and the means one should employ or accept, the *Living Flame* in both poem and commentary considers the end of the journey, the goal. In every sense the *Living Flame* is the peak of John's teaching. Unlike the *Spiritual Canticle* and the *Ascent-Dark Night* that are full of movement and progress, the *Living Flame* is not developmental and can seem static in comparison to the others. It presents a succession of parallel scenes without progress. However, it is filled with the tension and satisfaction of love and gives a deeper understanding and development of the love of encounter and union.

Like the *Song of Songs*—so dear to John—the "Dark Night" and the "Spiritual Canticle" are love poems. Many commentators feel these poems have no immediate religious dimension, but offer the longings of lovers for union. The commentaries are very different of course, in so far as they add a clear religious interpretation to the poems. At first reading the "Living Flame" seems different. While the "Spiritual Canticle" and to a lesser extent the "Dark Night" are love songs, filled with romantic and erotic language and themes, the "Living Flame" appears more as a religious poem, and the commentary certainly does. However, in the "Living Flame," John picks up themes and vocabulary that in contemporary Spanish poets were romantic and erotic, making the "Living Flame" a poem of loving union. Some English translations of the poem, that capitalize "You," and "Your," give a distracting overlay and religious interpretation where none exists in the original work.

The commentary on the *Living Flame* describes the depth of the love relationship in spiritual marriage. "[T]hese stanzas treat of a love deeper in quality and more perfect within this very state of transformation" (F. Prologue.3). It is different from the *Spiritual Canticle*, even though close in time and, to some extent, in thought. It describes situations outside our normal understanding of the stages in the spiritual life, while insisting that what it describes is not itself a stage, but rather four facets of the final encounter of spiritual marriage. The *Spiritual Canticle* emphasizes the role of Christ in the maturing of love in the journey to divine union, whereas the *Living Flame* emphasizes the role of the Holy Spirit as agent and guide of all the work of Christian holiness. In his earlier works John describes the purification and dismantling of a false self, false values, and false understanding of the focus of the intellect, will, and memory. Then in the *Spiritual Canticle* he presents the journey of two lovers to union. Now, in the *Living Flame* he looks at four aspects of the singular union achieved at the end of the *Spiritual Canticle*. First, he describes how a person is united in love with the Holy Spirit. Second, he stresses how a person is immersed in the life and love of the Holy Trinity. Third, he comments on how one is transformed by God's love and attributes. Finally, he shows how in spiritual marriage one understands the whole cosmos in union with the love of the Word. In the *Living Flame* John is not offering norms and guidance to get to the end. Rather, he is describing the nature of the end. He is introducing us to the meaning of human existence and the call of humanity to transformation in union with God.

The poem and commentary of the Living Flame

There are three phases in John's development of the *Living Flame*, as there are in the *Spiritual Canticle*. First he writes a poem, then he writes the commentary, and finally he revises the commentary, giving rise to a second redaction. John wrote the poem of the "Spiritual Canticle" for his own support and consolation in times of trial and suffering in the Toledo prison. He wrote the "Living Flame" at the request of Doña Ana de Peñalosa. John had first met this "very noble and devout lady" in 1582 when he arrived in Granada, accompanying a group of nuns to found a new monastery. The Archbishop had given his approval but then withdrew it, leaving the nuns without a place to set up their monastery. Doña Ana let them use her home. After John was made prior of Los Martires, he became spiritual director to the devout lady. In this poem John deals with the final expressions of love in mystical union precisely at the time he is being attacked by defamations from his enemies. The poem describes unceasing activity without progress. It is an interior revelation of varied perspectives; four phases of the inhabitation of the Trinity in the soul.

The title of the poem is taken from the first verse. The poem has four stanzas of six lines each instead of the usual five. John may well have taken the form of the stanzas from Garcilasco de la Vega's "Canción Segunda." John may have read Garcilasco's poems, some of which were published in 1536 by the wife of Boscán, and later Sebastián de Cordoba rewrote Garcilasco's poems, transposing them to a religious level.[8] John uses the longer stanzas to achieve the scope of his work. They are slower and richer, giving the impression of fullness and satisfaction. When one would expect the stanzas to end, they go on for another line, thus creating the dynamism of the abundant satisfaction of love.[9] The poem describes a state rather than a journey. It contains eight exclamations that substitute for statements, and they give the impression of the awesomeness of what he describes—the irrationality of the expressions of love. Although focused on the present joy of union with God, each of the first three verses has a retrospective line, as present joy reminds the person making the spiritual journey of previous suffering that led to this union. The last stanza, focused entirely on the present, is permeated with peace.

The commentary was written very soon after the poem. It is very close to the poem and more than a commentary, it seems a prolongation of the poem in its lyrical and mystical style, exclamations, and tensions of love. The first redaction was again for Doña Ana de Peñalosa and John completed it in two weeks. The second redaction would only come during the last months of John's life at La Peñuela. The second redaction revises the commentary on stanzas one, two, and three, while leaving stanza four practically the same. The second redaction is about one seventh longer than the first. The words and order are the same. John changes little, leaves out little, modifies a few things, and adds some explanations. John worked on the second edition from August to September of 1591 while in La Peñuela where he had gone after the Madrid Chapter of 1591.

The commentary follows the order of the four stanzas, and John uses the opportunity of the three retrospective lines to make long digressions on previous stages in the spiritual life (F. 1.18-26; 2.23-31; 3.18-67). The digressions, which are about a third of the work, are very helpful for those who have not reached this stage of union. While the poem is beautiful, many consider the commentary to be arid and find it the least interesting of John's works. Some suggest it is not as beautiful, complex, and exciting in its movements as the *Dark Night* and the *Spiritual Canticle*. The three large digressions can be confusing as they block the direct flow of the major theme. In the *Ascent* John spoke about obscure explanations, unpolished style, doubtful ability, and exceeding his own limits (A.2. 14.14). Certainly on most occasions John never exemplifies these failures, but here and there the *Living Flame* is not without some confusion. John's audience is still restricted and therefore his applications are narrow and not always helpful to the modern reader who is not as advanced as John presumes. Moreover, John holds some truths to be self-evident which are not to modern seekers; God is love, human beings can never be satisfied except in union with God, and the journey to God is by negation! A further distraction in reading the commentary is the long digression on spiritual direction; useful though it is, it seems misplaced.

The relationship of the Living Flame to John's other works

John's four major works deal with our journey to God. The *Ascent* and *Dark Night* use the image of the night and the painful climb of Mount Carmel and describe especially the journey of faith. The *Spiritual Canticle* and the *Living Flame* use matrimonial or nuptial imagery and emphasize the journey of love. John deals with these explanations of our journey to God in light of his understanding of God's journey of love to us which he describes in the nine "Romances." Our journey to God is modeled on God's journey to us, and John is always aware of God's strategy of love, both in coming to us and in drawing us to divine life. John is a wonderful spiritual guide, for by the time he writes, he already knows the major steps in our journey even though they may not be entirely predictable, nor identical for all. But a prudent guide like John knows the key moments in our journey to God; he already knows possible pitfalls, challenges, moments of rest, and the ecstasy of the end.

When John of the Cross writes any of his works his system of spiritual development is already complete, at least in his own mind. He may write other works later, but these are explanations for others not for him. John has a very clear understanding of the systematic development of the spiritual life and how each part relates to others in a progressive development. Part of John's genius is his ability to see the whole picture. So, when John writes to his directees he locates his advice within the context of the systematic development of the spiritual life (see L. 3 and 13, S. 19, 23, 25). In the *Spiritual Canticle* we meet the bride who already refers to the one she seeks as "him I love most." And she describes intense, loving union long before the spiritual betrothal. When she reaches an experience of union, she is told to go back to further purification. So, John sees the whole picture of the spiritual life and how each part fits in with the whole picture.

As already mentioned, the *Living Flame* is not progressive but describes four facets of the final stage of spiritual marriage. While it touches on themes already developed in the *Dark Night* and the *Spiritual Canticle* and uses lists of words and images from other poems, it is a new work altogether. The themes of light and darkness give way to flame and fire. The *Canticle* ends by commenting on "the serene night with a flame that is consuming and painless (stanza 39). The *Living Flame* deals with the end of the journey—the summit to which all else leads. It is the most complete of John's poems and commentaries and sets the whole spiritual journey in context. It gives the conclusion of the journey and thereby puts everything else in context—darkness, longing, pain, and negation find meaning in this poem's description of the end. Other works anticipate this one. In the poem, "Without support yet with support," which describes one's attitudes and commitment in the spiritual journey, John describes how love works in a person, leading him or her to transformation. He concludes, "And so in its delighting flame which I am feeling within me, swiftly, with nothing spared, I am wholly being consumed." In the *Spiritual Canticle's* last section that deals with the bride's longing for the deeper union of eternity, she says, "Let us rejoice, Beloved, and let us go forth to behold ourselves in your beauty. . . . There you will show me what my soul has been seeking. . . . in the serene night, with a flame that is consuming and painless" (verses 36, 38, 39). In the commentary, John states explicitly, "By the 'flame' she here understands the love of the Holy Spirit" (C. 39.14). Even the *Dark Night* anticipates the *Living Flame*, for "the 'Noche' is dark, but the darkness is joyful and affirmative, the 'Llama' is ardent but the flame wounds, and there has been darkness to negotiate before its light and heat can be felt."[10] When John describes the early experiences of love in the dark night of contemplation, he says, "The fire of love is not commonly felt at the outset, [but] In the measure that the fire increases, the soul becomes aware of being attracted by the love of God and enkindled in it. . . . At times this flame and enkindling increase to such an extent that the soul desires God with urgent longings of love" (N.1 11.1). In the second book of the *Dark Night* when John describes the nature of the passive night of spirit, he says, "the soul is purged and purified by this fire of love" and later "the fire of love returns to act more interiorly on the consumable matter of which the soul must be purified" (N.2. 10.6-7).

John's approach to the Living Flame

In his dedication to Doña Ana John tells us that the *Living Flame* is "a commentary on the stanzas which treat of the very intimate and qualified union and transformation of the soul in God." It is a description of the experiences of a person at the time of spiritual marriage. It is not a further stage in the spiritual life. Rather, "these stanzas treat of a love within this very state of transformation that has a deeper quality and is more perfect" (F. Prologue.3). So, the *Living Flame* describes the highest degree of perfection, the transformation in God, spiritual marriage, and divine union. It is a union through the likeness of love, the highest state attainable in this life. The *Living Flame* begins with full possession and uncontainable dynamism of a love in full force (F. 1.8). The focus of this poem and book is not purification, nor even union. It is the enjoyment, celebration, glorification, mutual refreshment, and renewal of love. It is a manifestation of the power and transforming love of God for the benefit of the person who has made the journey to spiritual marriage. While John insists that this experience is always proportioned to each one's capacity, it remains the peak of the journey. Moreover, in reading the *Living Flame* we discover that the reality of this experience of union is not just more than we thought it would be, it is of a totally different manner of union. In his introduction to the *Living Flame of Love* E. Allison Peers comments: "Yet it must be agreed that in the *Living Flame of Love*—the shortest of his four great treatises— St. John of the Cross takes us still farther into the mysteries of which he is so rare an exponent and presents us with a work, less tenderly appealing, no doubt, than the *Spiritual Canticle*, but written with a greater eloquence and ardour, impetuosity and lyrical fervor, telling of a love more completely refined and of a soul nearer than ever to God."[11]

Like the *Spiritual Canticle*, "these stanzas . . . were composed in a love flowing from abundant mystical understanding" (C. Prologue.2). John's teaching is always very demanding, but it deals with the demands of love. He wants people to love nothing but what God loves. In this poem and commentary, John describes the peak of the spiritual journey with the passionate expressions of the language of love. However, at the moment of encounter, John of the Cross, like all mystics, becomes silent. Having brought us so far they and he leave us a little empty, overwhelmed by the ineffable. "I do not desire to speak of this spiration, filled for the soul with good and glory and delicate love of God, for I am aware of being incapable of so doing, and were I to try, it might seem less than it is" (F. 4.17). Generally, a mystic longs to share with others his or her experiences as a sign of his or her love of God whose love they experience. They have a profound desire to express their experiences, and in doing so they enrich their own experiences. In the Toledo prison John experienced mystical union in love and felt the urge to share it in verses of the *Spiritual Canticle* that "were obviously composed with a certain burning love of God" (C. Prologue.1). Nevertheless, even in the commentary, John still evidenced reluctance to share on more intimate spiritual matters, feeling it was beyond human ability. "It would be foolish to think that expressions of love arising from mystical understanding, like these stanzas, are fully explainable" (C. Prologue.1).

John who did not seem to have inclination to write the commentaries generally did so only in response to frequent requests. In the prologue to the *Living Flame* John's reluctance to write becomes more clearly expressed. He says he lacks enthusiasm for the task, feels he is wanting in the needed communication skills, struggles to articulate his ideas, and even says he lacks the necessary motivation. When considering the first stanza John points out that he wants to use exclamations since he feels they will express more than logical statements. It is as if he wants to tell the reader that exclamations are as good as he can do! (F. 1.2). In the second stanza he tells the reader not to be amazed by what is happening to a person in this experience of union. Certainly it is beyond anything we can imagine, but God promised this, and so we should be ready for it (F. 2.36). In the same stanza he also speaks of his inability to fully describe what he wants to. "I would desire not to speak of it so as to avoid giving the impression that it is no more than what I describe" (F. 2.21). In the third stanza, John feels overwhelmed again. "May God be pleased to help me here, for I certainly need His help to explain the deep meaning of this stanza" (F. 3.1). In the final stanza, as we have seen, he again expresses his reluctance to talk about the intimate matters referred to in the poem. "I do not desire to speak of this inspiration, filled for the soul with good and glory and delicate love of God, for I am aware of being incapable of doing so, and were I to try, it might seem less than it is" (F. 4.17). Although John often expresses reservations about writing this book, nevertheless, he is also very concrete and practical in his explanations. He is the consummate teacher who wants to make sure his readers understand the main teachings.

John's mystical language and symbolism

It is always difficult if not impossible to express profound spiritual experiences in conceptual and speculative language. People who have had a profound spiritual experience generally find it difficult to explain it to others in precise language. Often this is because they do not fully understand it themselves, or their explanation always seems to fall far short of the experience. Even John mentions his inability to fully communicate his experiences, and simply refers to them as "stammerings." Because of this difficulty, mystics often use figurative expressions rather than rational explanations. John's major works begin with figurative titles— ascent, dark night, canticle of love, living flame—titles that already evoke responses in the hearts of believers. John then presents his poems as glimpses into his profound experiences: "unable to express the fullness of his meaning in ordinary words, [he] utters mysteries in strange figures and likenesses" (C. Prologue.1). When disciples ask John to explain these poems he starts with a prologue in which he states that it is not possible to explain adequately the experiences to which the poems refer. "I have felt somewhat reluctant . . . to explain these four stanzas. . . since they deal with matters so interior and spiritual, for which words are usually lacking. . . I find it difficult to say something of their content...." (F. Prologue.1; see also A. Prologue.1 and C. Prologue.2).

Given this drawback of ordinary language, mystics often choose poetry as a natural form to express the mysteries of God. Finding the experience ineffable, indescribable, mystics use the transformative and transcendent language of poetry which is generally synthetic, global, creative, and always open to new meanings at other times. In addition to poetry and hyperbole, mystics use symbols—images that bring together a set of characteristics and evoke a precise response. Sometimes images already have interpretations attached to them, as they do in John. For example the two lovers reflect the lovers of the *Song of Songs*, and cloud and darkness remind us of God's guidance of the chosen people during their wanderings in the desert. Examples of symbols in John would be fire, light, night, nature, and matrimony. John is well-known for his use of the symbol of the night which he uses 247 times. For John, night describes the whole spiritual journey: dark night, glad night, tranquil night, guiding night, serene night, night more lovely than the dawn, and night that has united the Lover with his beloved. However, John is also known for his use of matrimonial symbolism to describe the whole of the spiritual journey: early longings, lovesickness, companionship, engagement, and finally spiritual marriage.

The *Living Flame* contains romantic and matrimonial symbolism, but also uses the symbolism of the flame and fire that burn, purify, and transform, giving light and heat. "This flame of love is the Spirit of the Bridegroom, who is the Holy Spirit" (F. 1.3). The flame wounds and brings pleasure, it wounds in the deepest part of one's spirit—tenderly. It implies energy, causes love, and constantly enflames the person to bring love to others. Except for the three digressions, the image of the flame dominates the commentary even more than it does the poem. While it is the predominant symbol in the *Living Flame*, John had already used it elsewhere (see N.2. 12.5; C. stanza 39). "The *Llama* shows that in the end San Juan is not simply a negative theologian. The symbol of the 'llama' is in many ways the positive counterbalance to the 'noche'. The painful detachment required in the dark night is one and the same with the purgation by burning in the flame."[12] In the *Living Flame* we must remember that beyond the symbolism of fire, flame, touch, hand, there is always a person.

Necessary attitudes in reading the Living Flame

I have already mentioned the *importance of appreciating the entire spiritual system of John* when one chooses to read any of his works. Likewise an attentive reader must see the links between John's various works, know something of the historical background and times of John, and be sensitive to his use of mystical language. When reading John's works we must avoid entering them with prejudice from former false understandings of John. We should read his writings directly, often, and reflectively, and try to enter into dialogue with John. We should appreciate the unique focus and message of each of his works, remember the central significance of his poetry, and above all be sure to interpret his message for today.[13]

The *Living Flame* deals with the final experiences of the spiritual life prior to the total union with God in eternity. We can easily think that these experiences are unreal and the teachings too extraordinary for most human beings. Or at least we can conclude that reading the *Living Flame* is a waste of time for us who will never attain what John describes. John is aware of this possible response and warns readers against it. "There is no reason to marvel at God's granting such sublime and strange gifts to souls He determines to favor. If we consider that He is God and he bestows them as God, with infinite love and goodness, it does not seem unreasonable" (F. Prologue.2). It is important to *begin with an awareness of God's goodness and of the human call to greatness and to union with God in love.* We can always thwart our challenge to spiritual growth by insisting on a reduced ideal of our calling. John reminds us that God "declared that the Father, the Son, and the Holy Spirit would take up their abode in anyone who loved Him" (F. Prologue.2). So, in approaching this book, let us gratefully appreciate this call to humanity and be enthused by it even though we may still be at an earlier stage in the spiritual life.

When undertaking this journey we must not feel burdened by thoughts of the impossibility of making even the first steps. We are not struggling to move forward step by step. Rather *we must be aware that God is drawing us to divine life.* "In the first place it should be known that if a person is seeking God, his Beloved is seeking him much more" (F. 3.28). So, John urges an attitude of confident response. "The soul, then, should advert that God is the principal agent in this matter, and that He acts as the blind man's guide who must lead it by the hand to the place it does not know how to reach" (F. 3.29). The primary activity of one who seeks God is not to place any obstacles in the way of God's work of drawing the person to union in love.

A key attitude in one who makes this journey is to *want to reach the goal*. We need to desire intensely the transformation of our spiritual faculties, so that we can know and understand in a new way, love in a new way, and hope in a new way. We must yearn to know God in faith and not in the accumulation of knowledge, to possess God in hope and not in the accumulation of memories, and to love God in charity and not in the accumulation of desires. When a person empties these "deep caverns of feeling" "the thirst, hunger, and yearning of the spiritual feeling is intolerable" (F. 3.18). A lot of people say they want to pursue union with God but they do not have the necessary attitudes. We must match our longing with readiness to be drawn by God.

A person who wishes to undertake the journey to the union John describes, besides having the conviction just mentioned, must *maintain a spirit of deep recollection*. From the beginning of the book John tells us "one speaks badly of the intimate depths of the spirit if one does not do so with a deeply recollected soul" (F. Prologue.1). Reading the *Living Flame* requires education and sensitivity born of deep recollection. As John pointed out, "This spirit and life is perceived by souls who have ears to hear it, those souls, as I say, that are cleansed and enamored" (F. 1.5). In the second stanza John comments: "The appropriate language for the person receiving these favors is that he understand them, experience them within himself, enjoy them, and be silent" (F. 2.21). He elsewhere recommends a "deep and delicate listening" (F. 3.34). Dabbling in the spiritual life will get one nowhere in reading this book. John acknowledges that some people are just not ready for the material of this book. "Those who do not relish this language God speaks within them must not think on this account that others do not taste it" (F. 1.6). Only a total immersion in the desire for the will of God and longing for God's love will enable one to appreciate John's channeling of God's call to the enjoyment of union. John waited to write the commentary until he felt God has endowed him with gifts of knowledge and fervor. We will need the same gifts to read it with profit.

Perhaps the one great attitude needed to benefit from this wonderful book is that the person who seeks this transformation must above all *desire that God be everything* to his or her life. In the verses of the *Spiritual Canticle* that describe spiritual marriage (verses 22 and following), the bride says, "I gave myself to him, keeping nothing back." John comments, "[S]he most willingly and with intense delight surrenders herself wholly to him in the desire to be totally his and never to possess in herself anything other than him" (C. 27.6). This is a time when one who pursues God gives himself or herself totally with fidelity and stability, wanting nothing except what God wants and doing nothing except what God wants. So, the person now knows how to do nothing except love God, employing one's entire being in the pursuit of love. Stanza 28 sums up the approach of the person who seeks union with God. "Now I occupy my soul and all my energy in his service; I no longer tend the herd, nor have I any other work now that my every act is love." God is everything to the person who approaches this stage. It is a fundamental attitude of directing the whole of life to God and centering all one does on God alone. "Everything I do I do with love, and everything I suffer I suffer with the delight of love" (C. 28.8).

Finally, in reading any of John's works, we should *never be locked in to one interpretation*. It is important that we always let God speak to us according to the divine will for us. John gave the guidance for our approach to all his works in the prologue to the *Spiritual Canticle*. "As a result, though we give some explanation of these stanzas, there is no reason to be bound to this explanation. For mystical wisdom, which comes through love and is the subject of these stanzas, need not be understood distinctly in order to cause love and affection in the soul, for it is given according to the mode of faith through which we love God without understanding him" (C. Prologue.2).

CHAPTER FOUR
THE STORY OF THE LIVING FLAME OF LOVE —
a summary[1]

Prologue:

1.* John of the Cross tells Doña Ana de Peñalosa, for whom he has written the book, that he felt reluctant to write about the intimate and spiritual matters addressed. Moreover, he tells her he has put off writing it until the Lord gave him

---

[1] See *Collected Works of St. John of the Cross*, translated by Kieran Kavanaugh, O.C.D., and Ottilio Rodriguez, O.C.D., (Washington, DC: ICS Publications, 1991), *"The Living Flame of Love,"* pp. 577-649. This is an effort to summarize the book of the *Living Flame*; it is about one third of the original length. It leaves out asides and duplicate explanations, while faithfully presenting the words and ideas that John writes. There are still some problems with language and concepts that are unusual for contemporary readers. However, in a shorter version it still gives us chance to immerse ourselves in John's context, ideas, and spiritual challenges.

the appropriate recollection and insight to do so. He feels limited in his ability to deal with matters so sublime and vital, submits his work to the Church's judgment, and feels confident the reader will appreciate that what he says is a poor reflection of the spiritual realities.

2. God favors people with the sublime experiences here described, and tells us that the Trinity would dwell in those who loved God. 3. The *Spiritual Canticle* spoke of spiritual marriage—the highest stage of perfection in this life. This present poem treats of a very special quality of love within this final stage. In this life one cannot pass beyond spiritual marriage, but with time and practice, within spiritual marriage, one can experience a love that is deeper and more intense. 4. John describes the person who has reached this experience of inner transformation in which he or she feels united to the fire of love.

Stanza 1

O living flame of love

That tenderly wounds my soul

In its deepest center! Since

Now You are not oppressive,

Now Consummate! If it be Your will:

Tear through the veil of this sweet encounter!

Commentary. 1. Here one feels vigorously transformed, possessed by God, and inflamed in divine union, and senses that the union of eternity is but a step away as the love experienced bursts into flame. The soul asks that the Holy Spirit remove the last obstacle to total union.

2. *O living flame of love.* Filled with love, the person expresses with many exclamations intense desire and affection. 3. The flame of love is the Holy Spirit, a fire that consumes, transforms, and enflames. The soul, transformed in love, feels the activity of the Holy Spirit in two ways—as a permanent presence of transforming love and as an experience of enflamed love in the Spirit's acts within the soul. The former is a habit of love, the latter an act of intense love that is an effect of the habit. 4. The former is like a log burning intensely, the latter is like when a fire bursts into flame. The more intense is the fire the more vehemently will it burst into flame. Now, one can no longer act on one's own for the Holy Spirit acts within, so that all the person's acts are now divine, since they result from God's activity within the soul. So, the person experiences the enflaming love of the Holy Spirit, and tastes union with God in eternal life.

5. People who are cleansed and filled with love can hear the voice of God—the deeper and purer their love the clearer they can hear God communicating a foretaste of eternity. 6. This foretaste is not perfect, since that is impossible in this life. But, when the Holy Spirit causes a person to burst into the flame of love, he or she gains a taste of eternal divine love, lives in God, and experiences the living God. This is so intense an experience that the soul exclaims: O living flame of love!

7. *That tenderly wounds my soul.* The living flame of love touches a person so deeply he or she feels the pain of a wound of love and dissolves in love. 8. Of course, since the person has been totally transformed in love, one can ask "what is left to wound?" Love is never idle but always growing and bursting into flame, and as it does it causes further wounds of love in the depths of one's heart.

9. *In its deepest center!* This union of love takes place in the substance of the soul away from the influences of the senses or of evil. There, in the interior of a person, immersed in purity of commitment, God does all without the individual doing anything except to receive from God. God works in the depths of a person so that all activities are divine. 10. The human being is a spirit, thus has no parts, no qualitative differences, no degrees or perfection of intensity. 11. Here, the deepest center of a person is that point beyond which one no longer has further movement. It is at the furthest point of one's being and power. 12. The soul's center is God, and when it reaches God with all its being and strength it will love and enjoy God with all its might.

13. Love motivates a person to move to God—the deeper the love, the deeper one can center oneself in God. There are degrees of love as the person attains union, concentrates, and finally experiences the wounding that transforms the soul so it appears to be God. 14. When the flame of love wounds one in the deepest center it means the Holy Spirit has reached the soul's substance, power, and strength. A person rejoices in this fullness of communication and perfection in this life, aware that even greater communication comes in the next life. As one is transformed so the delight one feels is more intense and tender, and a person feels transformed in his or her deepest center.

15. These experiences seem incredible but God is generous in love. Once a person is purified, tried in the fire of tribulations, and found faithful in love, God promised the Trinity would come to indwell, illuminating and delighting the person. 16. The activity of the Holy Spirit within the soul is far greater than any other communication and transformation of love. If the latter resembles glowing embers, the activity of the Holy Spirit is like embers that have become so hot they shoot forth a living flame. The former is a union of love alone, the latter an enflaming of love that brings

a vision of peace, glory, and tenderness. 17. The soul feels that this living flame of love draws it to its greatest capacity and strength, communicates divine knowledge, and transforms the capacity of intellect, will, and memory. Thus, the Holy Spirit enflames the purified soul and the soul is absorbed in God.

18. *Since now You are not oppressive* (a digression, 18-26). When the soul was in the previous state of purification in contemplation, the flame of God's love was not experienced as friendly and gentle as it will become in spiritual marriage. 19 At that time, the Holy Spirit as the living flame sought the purification of all the person's imperfections in order to prepare him or her for the transformation in love that would come later. So, the fire of love that unites and transforms, previously purified. In this "purgative way" a person feels oppressed, as he or she suffers deprivations and afflictions of spirit. At this time the flame of love is not gentle but afflictive. The soul feels dryness, experiences darkness, suffers with self-knowledge, and feels wretched and distressed. 20. This is a time of trials in the intellect, dryness in the will, and burdensome knowledge in the memory. Oppressed by the purifying flame, a person finds no relief or consolation, rather oppression and abandonment. 21. These sufferings are intense, but this is the only way to purify the soul of all its weaknesses and to show the soul its profound need of transformation.

22. So, the living flame makes a person see and feel his or her own weaknesses. It seems there is a war going on between the virtues and goodness of God and the negative habits of the soul. The brightness of the flame throws light on the darkest regions of the soul, causing confusion and pain. At the same time the illuminating flame enables the eye of the soul to see what previously it could not. So, at this time the flame seems oppressive. 23. Although the flame is essentially loving, the soul is hard, dry, and unfeeling—totally

unprepared for loving union until the darkness, hardness, dryness, and lack of feeling for spiritual values are driven out. The flame overwhelms, enlarges, widens, and makes one capable of receiving love. A person experiences the flame's transforming actions as oppressive, unpleasant, and bitter, and sees nothing except his or her own weaknesses, misery, poverty, and evil. However, as God transforms the soul, he softens, pacifies, and clarifies it, preparing it for the union that lies ahead. 24. God allows this purification in varying degrees and intensity, according to the divine will for each one. It is a preparation for transformation.

25. The two books on *The Dark Night* and *The Ascent of Mount Carmel* dealt with the intensity of the purification of intellect, will, and memory, as well as all aspects of purification of both sense and spirit. In reviewing that material, it is worth remembering that the flame of love which in this present poem is gentle and transforming in loving union is the same flame that was formerly oppressive, as it assailed the person in periods of purification. 26. So, the phrase "Now You are not oppressive" means the flame is no longer dark but illuminating, no longer weakens in oppressive purification but strengthens in love, no longer heavy and constringent but liberating in its delight and fullness. (End of digression).

27. *Now Consummate! if it be Your will.* The person asks that spiritual marriage be complete in a union beyond this life. Although experiencing fullness of love he or she still yearns for what lies ahead. The present union is itself beyond what a human without God's help can sustain, but ahead lies a union in the sublime fire of glory and the person full of joy and love still feels personal incompleteness. 28. However, the soul does not experience pain, for more than anything else it finds joy in the fulfillment of God's will. Nevertheless, the living flame enflames the person with acts of love so intense that he or she cannot help looking ahead to the fullness of

union only now glimpsed. The communication of the Holy Spirit rouses and invites the person to maintain a focus on what lies ahead.

29. *Tear through the veil of this sweet encounter!* There are three veils which constitute a hindrance to total union, and these must be breached to achieve the union in love for which the soul longs. The first two—the temporal veil of creatureliness and the veil of all natural inclinations and operations—must be removed by renouncing all natural appetites and affections. This the flame achieves through spiritual purification. When these two veils are breached a person can be united to God in this life. In the period described in this poem only the third veil remains. This refers to death by which the soul can reach a union unattainable when bound by the restrictions of this life. This is not painful, but a sweet encounter.

30. Death for individuals in this stage does not result from sickness and old age (even if they may be sick or elderly). Rather, it results from a powerful encounter of love. Such a death is gentle, sublime, and delightful. 31. The person sees he or she is ready for union with God and knows the rich gifts received from God. Nothing is now lacking except to break through this third veil and leave behind the entanglements of this life.

32. There are three reasons for using the term "veil": first, it is a separation between spirit and flesh. Second, it refers to the separation between the soul and God. Third, a veil is thin and light can shine through it. The soul is transformed and can see the divinity shining through this last veil. Seeing the power of the other life, a person perceives the weaknesses of this one—everything else is without value, God alone is all. 33. This transformation results from a strong and impetuous touch of love, very brief and quick, done in an instant, an intense act in a short time, done without any long

immediate preparation. Thus, it is best described as the brevity of tearing than any other way.

34. The person wants no further delay and, moved by the force of love, begs that the veil of life be torn immediately. It seems that God takes before their time souls that love ardently, having perfected them in love in a short period. It is important for all of us to make such acts of love that we may prepare to see God. 35. The assault of the Spirit in this transformation in love is an encounter in which God undertakes to purify, perfect, penetrate, and absorb the soul in God. It is an encounter that is sweeter than all others. 36. This is a summary of the stanza that is remarkable in its clarity and challenge.

Stanza 2

O sweet cautery,

O delightful wound!

O gentle hand! O delicate touch

That tastes of eternal life

And pays every debt!

In killing You changed death to life.

Commentary 1. This stanza proclaims that it is the Holy Trinity who effects this divine work of union. "Cautery" that causes a wound refers to the Holy Spirit, the hand that gives a taste of eternal life to the Father, and the touch of transformation to the Son. These favors and blessings transform the soul in the Trinity.

2. *O sweet cautery.* This is the Holy Spirit, a powerful fire of infinite love that transforms the person into itself. He burns as he wills and according to each one's preparations. At times he touches vehemently with a burning stronger than all the fires of the world. In this burning the soul is enflamed and becomes itself a cautery of burning fire. 3. Although this fire is intense it does not consume or destroy or afflict the soul. Rather, it divinizes and delights it as it burns gently. The purpose of this burning is not to weary or restrict the soul but to enlarge and delight it for the burning is sweet.

4. The person in this experience knows all things, tastes all things, and does all it wishes, and prospers as he or she reflects on all the gifts received from God. 5. This is a wonderful blessing. It does not destroy the person but consumes in glory, filling with delight and wonder.

6. *O delightful wound!* The wound that is caused by the cautery is a wound of love that is delightful and sweet. 7. This wound of the flame of love also transforms any other wounds that come from miseries and sins. Generally a cautery leaves a wound, this cautery heals the wound by causing a deeper wound of love. As it wounds it cures and heals by causing a further wound. The deeper the soul's wound the healthier in love it becomes, for it is a delightful wound of the Holy Spirit.

8. The fire of love that is infinite delights and wounds according to the capacity of each person. Those who are wounded find delight and satisfaction in this affliction. This is truly a contemplative touch of the divinity caused by one who heals by wounding with love. 9. There are times when the person experiences a cautery in intellectual form—wonderful but not as deep as the cautery we have been considering. It seems an angel shoots an enflamed arrow of love. When the person is transpierced a vehement flame gushes forth and wounds the soul with unsurpassable delight. The person is

aware of this piercing, feels the point of the arrow in the depths of its spirit.

10. This point of piercing feels like the planting of a tiny seed that grows and spreads with the intensity of love throughout every part of the person. This flame of love strengthens, empowers, and imbues the soul with a sea of love. 11. Like the Gospel's mustard seed, this seed grows into a large tree, as the soul is overtaken with this immense love that emanates from the point of the arrow of love. 12. Few people reach these heights. God sometimes grants this to founders of communities or movements or people with lots of followers to spread this love to their disciples.

13. Returning to the piercing of the arrow, it can happen that God permits the intense effects on the soul caused by these wounds of love to extend and be experienced by the person's body. This is the case with those who receive the stigmata. Such wounds are without pain to the soul but can be painful to a corruptible body. When wounds are only in the soul they can be more intense. The outward manifestation in the body can restrain the intensity of love within.

14. Some think they can go to God relying on natural abilities, but one does not attain to the heights of the spiritual life without suppressing and leaving aside activities of the senses. However, it is a different thing altogether when the effect of the spirit overflows to the senses as we have just considered. 15. The cautery is wonderful. How wonderful too must be he who causes it.

16. *O gentle hand! O delicate touch.* The hand refers to the Father, generous and powerful, always ready to bestow gifts to the soul. This gentle and loving hand touches the person, bringing life and healing. This gentle hand of the Father wounds in order to heal, kills to give life. The only begotten Son of the Father is the delicate touch that wounds

and cauterizes to bring this healing love. 17. The Son of God subtly penetrates the substance of the soul, absorbing it entirely in delights and sweetness. The Son who is so awesome and mighty moves the person with a gentle and light touch. O Lord, the world does not appreciate the gentleness of your touch, but they who withdraw from the world and become mild find harmony in experiencing your mildness and gentleness. When they are refined, cleansed, purified and withdrawn from every creature you will dwell permanently in their souls.

18. Lord, you are strong and mighty, and you withdraw the person from all creatures by the might of your delicacy. Then the person finds no satisfaction in anything else except union in you alone. 19. The Word, immense and delicate, touches the pure soul that has capacity to receive it. The more abundantly the delicate touch pervades the soul the purer the soul becomes. 20. The delicate touch is indescribable, without form or figure, and simple. It is produced in the soul by the simple infinite being of God and touches subtly, lovingly, eminently, and delicately.

21. *That tastes of eternal life.* This touch is not yet perfect but anticipates eternal life. It is a touch of the substance of God in the substance of the soul. The effects are indescribable, and the person who receives this gift enjoys it in silence. It is a first taste of eternal life and of all the things of God. The soul enjoys in its substance all the qualities of God in one simple touch. 22. Sometimes, this experience of the touch of the Holy Spirit overflows to the body and sensory part. Thus, the body through this unction or anointing participates in the delights of the soul.

23. *And pays every debt!* (a digression 23-31). A person feels that the present delightful experience is a reward for the many trials it has endured in reaching this state. 24. Ordinarily, no one reaches this state of delight without having

passed through many tribulations and trials. These are now ended, for the person is purified and suffers no more. 25. These trials include temptations from the world, afflictions on the senses, and trials in the spirit. These purify a person in both sensory and spiritual parts. These trials are a necessary preparation for union. The person must be purified, strengthened, refined in sense and spirit for shorter or longer periods as God sees fit and according to the degree of union to which God wishes to raise the individual. 26. Through these trials and suffering a person acquires virtues, strength, and perfection.

27. Few people reach this high state described in this poem because God finds few who are willing to endure the purification. God gives little tests, finds that many cannot endure even these, and so proceeds no further. Many want to advance, pray to do so, but are unwilling to be guided in the suffering that leads to the advancement they seek. 28. Many people long to walk in security and consolation but cannot accept the purification. Only those who have served God, shown great patience and constancy, and have endured the trials God sends can advance along this road of denial, purification, and the cross. 29. This is how God acts towards those ready to be led to union. It is a journey of many purgations, each related to a further degree of love.

30. A person should never flee from these trials but face them with patience and constancy. These trials will be exterior and interior, spiritual and bodily, great and small. This is the way to combat evil habits and it will deaden evil, purify and strengthen the soul. People should rejoice in being chosen for this, for undergoing these trials is the way to a high state. 31. God repays these trials with divine goods for soul and body. This purification "pays every debt." (End of digression).

32. *In killing You changed death to life.* There are two kinds of life. The first consists in the vision of God attained by natural death. The second is perfect spiritual life acquired through the purification which we have considered. Without mortification one cannot attain the perfection of the spiritual life of union with God. 33. A person is unable to live the new life if the old life continues—focused on the world, indulgence of the appetites, and pleasure in creatures. In the new life faculties (intellect, will, and memory) are focused on God and appetites and activities become divine.

34. The transformed person lives the life of God. Thus, he or she has changed death to spiritual life. The intellect is no longer moved by natural light and senses but becomes divine in union with God. The intellect becomes one with God's intellect. The will's old forms of loving are changed into the life of divine love. God's will and the soul's will are now one. The memory no longer creates projections of the figures of creatures but is united to the mind and future of God. Natural appetites that used to relish creatures now find fulfillment in God alone. All movements and operations of the soul are now dead to their former life and alive to God and moved by the Holy Spirit. So the person becomes God through participation. Thus, the soul is dead to all it was in itself and alive to what God is in Himself, and the person can proclaim "In killing You changed death to life." 35. Such a person has left aside former life and is absorbed in divine life. 36. At this point he or she rejoices in the fruition and renewal God has brought. This transformation brings great merit to a person who celebrates the many gifts received. The individual feels God's constant solicitous love as if it were the exclusive object of God's love.

Stanza 3

O lamps of fire!

In whose splendors

The deep caverns of feeling,

Once obscure and blind,

Now give forth, so rarely, so exquisitely,

Both warmth and light to their Beloved.

Commentary 1. John requests God's help in explaining the deep meaning of this stanza. Readers need to be aware that if they have experience of these spiritual matters they will understand what follows, otherwise they will not. Here the person thanks the Beloved for graces received in this union, including knowledge, light, and love. What used to be obscure and blind can now receive illumination and warmth of love. The soul rejoices in giving back what it has received.

2. *O lamps of fire!* Lamps give light and heat, and these lamps shine and burn within the soul. Here, they refer to the many attributes of God. God is all these attributes in simple oneness of being. God discloses the divine life to the person in each of these descriptors or attributes. Each of these lamps in the soul gives forth light and warmth. 3. The soul experiences these attributes in one simple act of union. Thus, God becomes many lamps in the person, each one distinctly and altogether giving knowledge and enflaming him or her in love. God's omnipotence becomes a lamp of omnipotence, sharing and bestowing all knowledge. God as wisdom becomes a lamp of wisdom in the soul. Likewise, the divine

attributes of goodness, justice, fortitude, mercy, and all others communicate light and envelop the soul in love, so the person experiences all these attributes vitally.

4. Moses on Mount Sinai experienced the sublime and wonderful attributes of God. 5. The person delights in this embrace of love. Each lamp burns in love and enlightens and enflames all the other lamps. Thus, the person enjoys all attributes together and each one separately but always enriched by all the others. Absorbed, enflamed, and wounded by all these lamps together, the person becomes more alive in love and perceives that love is the essential aspect of eternal life. 6. All these lamps illumine in a friendly and loving way, enriching and delighting the soul. God communicates the divine life to the soul's faculties through the revelation and experience of the divine attributes. Each one loves and does good to others according to one's own nature and qualities. God who is omnipotent loves omnipotently. God is wise and loves with wisdom. God is infinitely good and loves with goodness. God is holy and with holiness loves. Likewise, God loves with the full power of all the divine attributes. Thus, God is just, merciful, liberal, absolute humility, and so on, and loves with the fullness of each of these qualities, revealing the divine self and communicating the divine self in this union.

7. Who can express the experience of such a happy person who is and feels loved and exalted in this way? The Beloved communicates knowledge of his graces and virtues, and the person is engulfed in these blessings. Thus, the soul rejoices in this whole harmonious composite and even the body feels this joy. 8. The person overflooded with these blessings of the flame finds that the flame is gentle even though it is an immense fire. It satisfies the thirst of the spirit, for these lamps also act like living waters. The Spirit of God is like soft refreshing waters which satisfy the thirst of the spirit and is also like living flames of fire that engulf the soul in love. This stanza deals with an indescribable experience and

the description falls far short of the reality. The person's transformation through participation in God and in God's attributes leads to the soul's union in divine life becoming God through participation.

9. *In whose splendors.* The splendors are the loving knowledge that God's attributes give forth to the soul and when united with the soul's faculties make the soul resplendent. Material lamps shed light around them, whereas the lamps of God's love give illumination within the flames. The person experiences illumination when in union within the lamps, and there it is transformed in each of the lamps.

10. The experience of the attributes of God illumines the person's faculties. The results of these experiences are not produced only by the soul, nor yet only by the Holy Spirit, but by both together, bringing transformation and glory to the soul. The Holy Spirit who is always wanting to bestow eternal life on the soul and transport it to glory in God grants many gifts in order to lead the person to life. The Holy Spirit does this gradually, until the appropriate time arrives for one's departure from this life. 11. These gradual movements are part of life. There is no movement or change in God. In this life it seems God is moving in the soul, but it is the soul that moves. Eventually, there comes a time when the soul moves no more for it is in perfect union.

12. The splendors—the loving knowledge that comes from experiencing God's attributes—can also be called "overshadowings" for through them God casts a shadow of protection over the person. 13. The object that casts a shadow produces different kinds of shades according to its nature— large, opaque, transparent, and so on. 14. Thus, the shadow that the lamps of God's beauty cast over the soul will be another beauty based on God's beauty, of God's fortitude another fortitude, of God's wisdom another wisdom, and so on with the other attributes or lamps. Since a person cannot

comprehend God fully in this life, it will always be a shadow of God's beauty, wisdom, fortitude, and so on. However, the soul will recognize that the shadow cast is clearly God's shadow.

15. The person experiences God in the divine attributes—referred to as splendors or shadows. The person understands and experiences God in each of these splendors or shadows—a shadow of omnipotence, wisdom, goodness, and so on. The person experiences God resplendent in these lamps through the splendors they produce or the shadows they cast. 16. John points out how the prophet Ezekiel had similar experiences. The person becomes extremely happy in this exaltation, overwhelmed by the splendors of God. 17. The divine attributes are simple being and are enjoyed in God distinctly, each one as enkindled as the other, and each substantially the other. Each one is known and enjoyed so as not to hinder the perfect knowledge and enjoyment of the other. Yet, each one throws light on the others.

18. *The deep caverns of feeling* (a long digression 18-67). The caverns are the soul's faculties of memory, intellect, and will. We know how they suffer when empty, and can appreciate how they rejoice when filled. When these caverns are not emptied of every affection, they do not appreciate their own capacity. Without purification any little thing can burden and bewitch them. Yet until they are completely emptied they cannot be filled. When they are empty and pure they feel intense pain at their own emptiness and yearn for what they lack, namely God. This painful experience of emptiness and longing normally occurs towards the end of a person's illumination and purification, just before reaching union. When the spiritual appetite is emptied of all affection for creatures and the soul still lacks communication with God in union, then the pain of emptiness is intense, and becomes even worse when now and then the person catches a glimpse of the union that lies ahead.

19. The intellect thirsts for divine wisdom. 20. The will hungers for the perfection of love. 21. The memory seeks the possession of God. 22. The capacity of these caverns—the spiritual faculties—is very deep because their true object is God who is profound and infinite. Their yearning for fulfillment in God thus becomes an infinite longing of intense pain. This suffering lies in the will's love, and love cannot alleviate this pain but only contribute to intensifying the longing. Only the possession of the Beloved alleviates the pain.

23. However, if the soul desires God fully it already possesses God. So, how can it suffer the want of what it already possesses? This desire for the vision of God contains no pain, since the soul possesses God in its desire. The more a person desires God, the more he or she possesses God, and this possession delights the soul. Thus, the greater a person's desire for God the greater the satisfaction and delight rather than pain and suffering. 24. Possession of God can be through grace or through union. The latter includes communication. The former is spiritual espousal, the latter spiritual marriage. The period of espousal includes purification, visits by the Beloved, gifts, and the complete "yes" of the soul to the will of God. The soul's will and God's will are now one, and thus the person attains possession of God by will and grace.

25. This is not comparable to spiritual marriage. To attain this latter the soul needs God to purify, beautify, and refine it so as to prepare it for union. This takes time depending on each one. 26. During this time of espousal the preparations of the Holy Spirit become more sublime and the caverns of the faculties experience extreme and delicate longing for fullness. Desire for God is more refined and profound, as a person prepares for union.

27. When God bestows these gifts on people, they need to be prudent, watching what they do and who they choose as

a spiritual director. 28. First, if a person is seeking God, he or she needs to be aware that God is seeking more than they. When a soul directs its desires to God, then God gives grace to draw the soul to divine life. Thus, God prepares a person until he or she merits union in God and transformation of spiritual faculties. 29. A person must realize that God is the principal agent in advancement. The person's responsibility is not to place any obstacles in God's way of guiding it. He or she must not be influenced by a blind guide. There are three blind guides who can lead the soul astray: the spiritual director, the devil, and the soul itself.

30. Since a disciple will become like the master, each one must choose a spiritual director very carefully. It is difficult to find an accomplished guide for all the stages of this experience. The spiritual director must be learned, discreet, and have the experience of a true and pure spirit. 31. Many spiritual directors harm souls, often because they do not understand the ways of the spirit. They misunderstand the graces of the Holy Spirit and instruct their directees in matters for beginners rather than seeing the call to greater union. So, they maintain their directees in the ways of beginners which is often all the director knows. Thus, some people cannot make progress. 32. Beginners emphasize meditation and acts of discursive reflection. The director should encourage these devotions. The directee profits from spiritual things and is attracted to them from the delight and satisfaction of the senses. Focused on spiritual things the appetite is torn away from sensual things and things of the world. Once a person becomes accustomed to spiritual things and endowed with fortitude and constancy, God weans the person away from the focuses of beginners and places him or her in the state of contemplation. This happens when the person finds it hard to meditate and finds no further satisfaction in it but only dryness. At this time God becomes the agent and the person the receiver. God works in those

who remains passive, and in contemplation grants them a loving knowledge.

33. At this time a person should be guided in a manner entirely different than formerly. The directee should stop meditating and the director should stop providing materials for meditation. At this point the person has lost the satisfaction found in meditation, now he or she should not even seek such satisfaction. If the directee focuses on satisfactions in the senses, he or she blocks the peaceful and quiet good God is giving to his or her spirit. Directors should not oblige directees either to meditate or to make acts of prayer or strive for fervor, for such activities become an obstacle to God's work within the soul, because God is passively bestowing wisdom and knowledge. The person should passively remain in God with a loving attention.

34. God and the soul commune through simple loving knowledge and attention. The person in order to receive these blessings must leave aside all natural manner of acting. If a person decides to act on his or her own, he or she would utterly hinder God's communications. At first such communications come with interior purgation and only later in the delight of love. The person receives this loving knowledge passively and not according to natural active ways of a soul. To achieve this approach a person must purify his or her natural operations and become quiet, peaceful, serene, detached from satisfactions—sensory or spiritual. So, no meditation, no attachments, no satisfaction, for all these impede, distract, and disquiet a person.

35. When a person is conscious of being placed in this solitude and spiritual listening, the person should even lay aside the practice of loving attention to be available for whatever God desires. The person should return to the practice of loving attention when he or she no longer experiences the inner idleness of spiritual listening. A soul can

recognize this change when it feels a certain peace, calm, and inward absorption. 36. Once drawn to contemplation a soul should no longer meditate, nor seek spiritual satisfactions, but remain detached from everything to receive God's communications passively.

37. Only when one is silent and detached can he or she receive God's communications. 38. Such a person leaves aside any former dependence on senses, passes through the trials of the desert, purifies those poor experiences and satisfactions that pass away so quickly. At this time the spiritual director should help the person to become detached from all satisfaction, relish, pleasure, and spiritual meditations. The director should not disquiet the person with cares concerning heavenly things and still less earthly things. But, bring such a person to complete withdrawal and solitude on the way to idle tranquility. Then God will infuse the spirit of divine wisdom that is loving, tranquil, solitary, peaceful, mild, and an inebriator of the spirit. In this the soul feels carried away by a spirit outside itself without contributing anything.

39. God's work at this time of holy idleness is beyond what we can imagine. The person is often unaware of what is happening but feels a sense of withdrawal and estrangement from all creatures and an inclination towards solitude in the love and life of the spirit. 40. These blessings are inestimable, hidden anointings of the Holy Spirit, secretly filling the person with spiritual gifts. 41. The soul and its spiritual director rarely comprehend these sublime gifts; only God the giver of these anointings understands. The person must not disturb these gifts by even the least act of memory, intellect, or will, or by any act of his or her own. This is a time to passively receive.

42. The harm done by interfering in this period of blessing can be immense. It might not be seen immediately but in the long term it is ruinous. 43. Causing this kind of

damage is common, and hardly any spiritual director avoids it. In this beginning of contemplation God blesses the person with loving knowledge that is serene, peaceful, and solitary, and the person withdraws from the senses, leaves aside meditation, and all sense satisfaction. At this time incompetent spiritual directors stunt the progress by urging the directee back to "useful" active meditation.

44. In contemplation the activity of the senses and discursive meditation end, and God now becomes the sole agent who leads the solitary and silent soul. Some spiritual directors without knowing sufficiently about the stages of prayer fail to see this and turn the person back to re-live the stages already passed and achieved. Once a person has reached quiet recollection in which the functioning of the faculties cease, it is not only useless to repeat the process to attain recollection it would also be harmful and a great distraction.

45. Some spiritual directors do not understand the nature of recollection and solitude, so they impose on the directee lower spiritual exercises, rather than let God work supernaturally. By this activity of natural operations a person loses the inner solitude and recollection God was achieving. 46. Spiritual directors should always acknowledge that the Holy Spirit is the soul's principal guide. The director's role is not to accommodate people to his or her methods but to observe the road along which God wishes to lead them. If he or she cannot see this, he or she should leave the directee alone. The director can contribute by leading a person into greater solitude, tranquility, and freedom of spirit, so when God introduces a person into contemplation, he or she does not remain attached to anything nor anxious when nothing seems to happen. At this time the soul is not doing anything, but God is. The director leads a person to complete detachment of sense and spirit and to emptiness, so that he or she can be ready for the silent and secret communications of

God. 47. The director's role is to help people ready themselves for God's communications. This is done in nakedness and emptiness of sense and spirit. So the director helps the person to purify natural operations and affections which cannot lead to God but only impede the process. The director's work is only preparatory. He or she should not get caught up in doing and getting the soul to do things. The soul accomplishes a lot when it learns how to do nothing; then it is ready to advance. For example, if it empties the intellect of knowledge, spiritual and natural, it becomes free to receive new knowledge from God.

48. Some say if the intellect does not understand something it does not make progress. This is not so. When it has knowledge it does not advance, for God transcends the intellect and is incomprehensible to it. When the intellect is active it is withdrawing from God. The intellect must withdraw from its normal object of knowledge so as to journey to God in faith. A person is united to God in faith and not in knowledge. When the intellect becomes empty it can advance by focusing itself in faith. At first this is darkness to the intellect, for the intellect cannot know God but must journey in submission in faith.

49. However, the will can only love what the intellect understands. True. But in contemplation there are no discursive acts. God in one act communicates light and love which is loving supernatural knowledge. This is contemplative knowledge which is dark to the intellect. Likewise, love is present in the will without specific objects or parts. God informs both intellect and will with knowledge and love. While these two faculties generally go together, God sometimes communicates more intensely with one or the other—communicating all knowledge or all love. So it is possible that God enflames the will in love without the intellect understanding.

50. Sometimes the will feels enflamed in love without understanding it. The will does not need to feel idle at this time. It does not need to make acts of love, for God takes over and fills it with divine love. 51. God does this only when the will is empty of other loves. As previously with the intellect, the will advances when it is empty of other loves. If the will does not go back to former loves, it advances, even though it does not experience God in a particular way. It enjoys God in the general infusion of divine love. In solitary quietude the soul loves God above all else that is loveable. It makes progress only when it does not and cannot dwell on any other object of love. It is now detached from its normal objects, so it can love or let God love in it. 52. Similarly, the memory detaches itself from all forms and figures in the imagination for God cannot be possessed in this way. When completely empty the memory can be filled with the future of God.

53. When people are in this emptiness some spiritual directors think they are idle, and they hinder their peaceful contemplation by urging them back to discursive meditation and interior acts. Those who have found this emptiness find this advice repugnant. These directors then urge them to renew fervor in their spiritual endeavors. These directors should be counseling exactly the opposite for these people have passed beyond these early stages. This misdirection can do harm—directees lose ground and suffer needlessly.

54. These spiritual directors do not know what the spirit is and show disrespect to both God and to the soul by intruding where they should not. God graces the soul bringing it to solitude and emptiness regarding faculties and activities, for God wants to speak to people's hearts. Reigning in a person in calm and peace God takes the initiative and feeds the soul without the activity of the senses. God values this passivity, tranquility, and solitary sleep, and forgetfulness. Incompetent directors do not like people to be at rest but prefer activity which ruins God's work. 56.

Directors may make these mistakes with good will, but they should learn more about this road to God, stop meddling, and leave the matter to someone who knows what he or she is doing. Reckless mistakes have a price to pay. God's affairs must be handled with tact and awareness, for great harm results when the director is wrong.

57. Some directors are full of vanity in guiding people. On this road individuals must change their style and mode of prayer and be introduced to sublime doctrine. Not everyone understands the stages of the spiritual journey or how to guide a person through the states of the interior life. When a director vainly thinks he or she has all the answers he does harm and hinders what God seeks to do in a person. Each one should know his or her own skills and limitations. 58. Some can guide a soul in mortification and contempt of the world. Others can introduce a soul to meditation. Others are needed to lead the soul to perfection and restful acceptance of God's work within. If the director binds the person to his or her own teaching that person does not advance for the path is blocked.

59. Maybe some directors can guide some people but not all in the same way, for God leads each one by different paths. When directors hold on to their directees they deprive them of their freedom and they act with arrogance and jealousy motivated by pride. 60. God becomes indignant with such directors. 61. Directors should give freedom to directees and encourage their desires for improvement. They do not know how God wants to lead a soul especially when the directee is dissatisfied with the director's teaching. This dissatisfaction is a sign that God is leading by a different path and the director should encourage the change.

62. One of the worst traits of incompetent directors is blocking God's efforts to urge a person to renounce the world, to change his or her way of life, and to serve God alone. Directors make matters worse for such people. They

themselves do not enter by the narrow gate and they force directees to stay away from the only path they should follow. Thus, they hinder the work of the Holy Spirit and will be punished since this is their duty and they should understand what they are doing.

63. The second blind guide capable of thwarting the soul's recollection is the devil. When one has withdrawn from creatures and receives the anointing of the Holy Spirit the devil is filled with sadness and envy, and strives to intrude in this withdrawal by striving to make the soul revert to the work of the senses. He distracts the soul, drawing it out of solitude and recollection. Some people who do not understand the road they are travelling easily incline to sensible satisfactions and the knowledge provided by the devil, and thus lose the solitude God provides. For small satisfactions one impedes God's work in solitude, thinking that doing something is better than waiting in solitude for God's anointing. 64. The devil with very little causes harm to a person alluring him or her away from solitude. Few people avoid this bait that the devil provides at the passage from sense to spirit as he deceives the soul by feeding the sensory part with sensible things. The person fails to see the potential loss and thus also fails to enter sublime recollection. If the devil fails in his effort he strives to make the person revert to sense by horrors, fears, bodily pains, noise—anything to draw the soul away from the interior spirit. Unfortunately, the devil finds blocking a person's enrichment in solitude easy and he accomplishes it with little effort. 65. People drawn to God in solitude and recollection should withdraw from all labors of the senses. Formerly this may have helped, now it is an obstacle. God is now the primary agent, and the soul needs to live in detachment and freedom of spirit so as not to impede its peace and tranquility.

66. The third blind guide is the soul itself by not understanding itself. Since it is accustomed to acting by

means of the senses and discursive recollection, it now thinks it is doing nothing when God introduces it into emptiness and solitude. When in the idleness of spiritual peace, the soul feels empty and is filled with dryness and displeasure. God wants the soul in silent quietude but the soul desires to act through its own efforts with the intellect and imagination. 67. A person should note even though he or she does not seem to be making progress in this quiet solitude he or she is advancing well. Although doing nothing with his or her faculties, God is achieving a lot, even though the person does not realize it. So, the soul should abandon itself to God, and God as the primary guide will assure advancement. (End of the digression).

68. When God anoints the deep caverns of the faculties—intellect, will, and memory—the suffering can be intense. God penetrates the very substance of the soul with these sublime anointings to prepare the faculties for union with God in spiritual marriage. At that time the satisfaction, fullness, and delight of the faculties will be great when they are transformed by the possession of divine knowledge, love, and glory. 69. Through the three faculties the soul experiences and enjoys the objects of the spiritual faculties, the grandeurs of God's wisdom and excellence. Through these deep caverns of feeling (the faculties) one has power and capacity for experiencing, possessing, and tasting the deep knowledge and splendors of the lamps of fire.

70. *Once obscure and blind.* Before God enlightens and illumines the soul, it dwells in obscurity, and when it is in sin it is blind, and even though God's light shines on it, it cannot see it. 71. A person is blind in total darkness because of sin, but one can be in obscurity without sin. Before reaching union a person was in obscurity regarding natural and supernatural things. Without the Lord's light, darkness covers the caverns (faculties) of the person's feelings. The soul cannot raise its eyes to God's divine light, when it has never

seen it before. It naturally desires only darkness because it knows what it is—going from darkness to darkness guided by darkness. With the light of God's grace the soul is transformed and illumined so that God's light and the soul's light become one.

72. The person was also blind when its appetites acted like a cataract allowing him or her to only see a little of the divine riches and beauty. Even a small appetite obstructs the clear vision of divine grandeurs. 73. It is impossible for a person with appetites to judge the things of God as they are. These appetites and satisfactions must be totally rejected for they impede knowledge of higher things. When a cataract covers the eye, a person only sees the cataract. Likewise, a person will infallibly come to consider the things of God as impertinent to God and the things impertinent to God as belonging to God. 74. So, people who have not purified their appetites and faculties consider some base things as highly important and some things precious to the spirit as of little value.

75. It is true that a person's desire for God is not always supernatural. In fact, a desire for God can be a natural appetite and remains such until God informs it supernaturally. When a person becomes attached to the satisfaction of spiritual things this is a natural appetite and it is a cataract in front of the eye of faith. In such a situation a person cannot understand or judge spiritual things. 76. So, the soul was once obscure without divine light, blind through its appetites and affections. Now with its faculties it has become bright and resplendent.

77. *Now give forth, so rarely, so exquisitely, Both warmth and light to their Beloved.* When the faculties are pervaded with the illumination of the lamps of fire, they give loving glory to God and surrender themselves to God. Having become enkindled lamps themselves, they give back the light

they have received. 78. The intellect receives divine wisdom "so exquisitely" and returns it to God in the same excellence. It also receives goodness in excellence and returns it in excellence. So, according to the excellence of the divine attributes that the Beloved communicates corresponds the excellence with which the soul gives back. In union the soul is now God through participation. Thus, through the substantial transformation the soul performs to God as God does in it. As God gave self totally, so the soul gives itself totally to God. The person is conscious of his or her inheritance as an adopted child, and having received God's gift of divine life, can give this gift of God back to God and to whomever he or she wishes.

79. In this way the person can offer to God the gift of the Holy Spirit, as if this gift were its own. Thus, the person gives to God all that God gave and thereby repays love with a suitable gift. God accepts this gift gratefully, as if the soul were giving something of itself—even greater than itself. Thus, God re-surrenders to the person, and the person loves God as if again. This reciprocal love is like a spiritual marriage in which the goods of each are possessed by both. This wonderful transformation is not as perfect as in the next life.

80. So, the soul can now give to God more than in itself it is worth. The presence of the Father, Son, and Holy Spirit is light and life within it, and by means of a highly illumined faith the soul gives this back to God. 81. The person makes this surrender with great refinement. The person enjoys fullness in the union of the intellect and affection with God and surrenders itself to God in wonderful ways. 82. Concerning love, first, the person loves God not through itself but through God, loving through the Holy Spirit as the Father and the Son love each other. Second, the soul also loves God in God, for the soul is now absorbed in God. Third, the soul loves God on account of who God is—not because God is generous or glorious, but because God is all this in essence.

83. Regarding fruition and fullness, one now enjoys God by means of God, since its intellect is now united to all the attributes of God. Second, the person enjoys God directly without intermingling of creatures. Third the person enjoys God because of who God is without its own pleasure. 84. The soul praises God excellently. First, because it is its duty, second, for the gifts it has received, and third because of who God is without any thought of benefit. 85. The soul expresses the excellence of gratitude: first for all natural and spiritual goods it has received, second because it finds great delight in praising God, and third, because of who God is.

Stanza 4

How gently and lovingly

You wake in my heart,

Where in secret You dwell alone;

And in Your sweet breathing,

Filled with good and glory,

How tenderly You swell my heart with love.

Commentary 1. The person here addresses the Bridegroom with deep love, thanking him for the effects produced by him from this union. 2. The first effect is an awakening of the spirit in gentleness and love. The second is the breathing of God in the person. 3. So, the person experiences an awakening of love in the very center and depths of his or her being. Here, in its intimate substance, the person knows the Lord is dwelling secretly and silently. The person feels captivated and aroused in love.

4. *How gently and lovingly You wake in my heart.* This elevated and beneficial awakening is a movement of the Word in the very substance of the soul, so filled with grandeur and glory that it seems the whole world participates in this intense movement of love. The Lord of the world united to the entire cosmos graces the person with love. 5. In this movement everything in the world discloses its beauty to the person, and he or she appreciates how all creatures find their life and strength in the Beloved. The person is aware that all creation is distinct from God, but now knows all things better in God's being than in themselves. Here is the delight of this awakening: the soul knows creatures through God and not God through creatures. The soul knows the effects through their cause and not the cause through its effects.

6. God renews the person so that he or she might behold this supernatural sight. God reveals to the person the divine life and being and the harmony of every creature in that divine life. In this movement the person is moved and awakened from the sleep of natural vision to supernatural vision. 7. The person sees what God is in essence and what God is in all the creatures of the world. By divine power, presence, and substance God holds them all in being. Through this cosmic awakening, God removes some of the veils that block this vision from the soul, so that the person may see God and God in creation at least partially.

8. When we are careless and asleep in God's presence we tend to think that God is also asleep and neglectful of us. 9. Yet everything comes from God, and we can do nothing of ourselves. This awakening of the soul is God's awakening within us. When God awakens and enlightens us we know and love the blessings that God presents to us. 10. What a person knows and experiences of God in this awakening is beyond words. It is the communication of God's excellence to the substance of the soul. The soul is established amidst infinite excellences and virtues—a terrible and solid array, but

the person is made gentle and charming with all the gentleness and charm of creatures. 11. Of itself, a person does not have the capacity and strength to deal with such glory. Here the person faces God filled with the graces of all creatures, awesome in power, glory, and excellence.

12. There are two reasons why a person does not become afraid in this awakening. First, he or she in this state of perfection is highly purged, is in conformity with the spirit, and is disposed to receive spiritual communications, and so does not feel the pain normally experienced by unpurified souls. Yet some suffering is still experienced in this overwhelming communication. The second reason is that God reveals the divine life gently. As God manifest the divine grandeur, God fortifies the soul's sensory part so that it does not know whether what is happening is in the body of out of it. So, the person experiences as much gentleness and love as he or she does power and grandeur. 13. The person no longer fears, for God acts in a friendly way towards it. God reveals divine power with love and goodness. God communicates strength and love, admirable virtues, charity, knowledge of higher and lower substances, and transforms the soul with the attributes of God.

14. *Where in secret You dwell alone;* The person feels God dwells in secret for God dwells in the very substance of the soul. But God dwells in souls in different ways. In some alone in others not alone, in some who please in others who do not, in some as in one's own home in others like a stranger. God dwells more in secret and alone when the soul has controlled all appetites and affections for creatures. Here God dwells with an embrace that is close, intimate, interior, and pure. The person experiences this intimate embrace sometimes in enjoying God in quiet sleep sometimes in an awakening when God communicates knowledge and love. 15. He or she is happy when experiencing God resting and reposing within. Such a person should withdraw from all

business matters and live in immense tranquility so that nothing may disturb the union with the Beloved. God dwells in the substance of the soul as if asleep, awakening now and again. Were God to be permanently awake in the soul it would already be in glory. 16. God dwells in other people who have not reached this union but God's dwelling is secret to them. Now and again they may feel an awakening, but it is not the kind we have been describing, because they have not yet controlled all affection for creatures. However, in the perfect soul all is perfect, and the awakening and in-breathing of the Holy Spirit is strangely delightful.

17. *And in Your sweet breathing, Filled with good and glory, How tenderly You swell my heart with love!* John says he feels incapable of describing this experience. God breathes the Holy Spirit into the soul and produces an awakening of divine knowledge, thus absorbing the soul in God and rousing its love. This breathing of the Holy Spirit fills the person with good and glory and enkindles him or her in love of God, to whom be honor and glory forever and ever. Amen.

* The numbers used throughout this summary correspond to the individual paragraph numbers of each section of the *Living Flame.*

CHAPTER FIVE
UNITED IN LOVE WITH THE HOLY SPIRIT (Stanza 1)

Overview of the stanza

The first stanza of the "Living Flame of Love" describes how a person is united in love with the Holy Spirit, feels completely transformed, possessed by God, inflamed in divine union, and close to the union of eternity. The person asks that the Holy Spirit remove the last obstacle to total union.

> O living flame of love
>
> That tenderly wounds my soul
>
> In its deepest center! Since
>
> Now You are not oppressive,

Now Consummate! If it be Your will:

Tear through the veil of this sweet encounter!

In the stage of spiritual marriage, which John of the Cross describes in the *Living Flame of Love*, the living flame is the Holy Spirit, who in this stanza, is a fire that consumes, transforms, and enflames a person. Such a one, transformed in love, feels the activity of the Holy Spirit in two ways—as a permanent presence of transforming love and as an experience of enflamed love in the Spirit's acts within the person. The former is a habit of love, the latter an act of intense love that is an effect of the habit.

This union of love takes place in the substance[14] of a person, in the very depths of the human spirit. There, in the transformed interior of a person, God does everything, without the person doing anything except to receive from God. God works in the depths of the person, in his or her very center, so that all activities become divine. Thus, the Holy Spirit enflames the purified person and transforms him or her in love by means of extraordinary communications. The person rejoices in this fullness of communication and perfection and is absorbed in God.

[There follows a digression, F. 1.18-26, which is presented here in chapter 2].

In this present state of spiritual marriage and fullness of love, the person longs for a union beyond this life, for he or she still feels incompleteness and yearns for the fullness of love the Lord alone brings. However, the person no longer experiences pain in this longing, for more than anything else he or she finds joy in fulfilling God's will. Moreover, the Living Flame enflames the person with acts of love so intense that he or she cannot help looking ahead to the fullness of union that is only now glimpsed. The Holy Spirit rouses and invites the person to maintain a focus on what lies ahead.

A person can only reach the next step of union through death which is not painful, but a sweet and powerful encounter of love. He or she is ready for union with God, feeling richly endowed by God, and aware that nothing is now lacking except to break through this final veil and leave behind the entanglements of this life. Transformation from this life to the next results from a strong and impetuous touch of love. It is an intense act in a short time, done without any long immediate preparation. The person wants no further delay and, moved by the force of love, begs that the veil of life be torn immediately. So, this first stanza describes the role of the Spirit in this transformation in love. It is an encounter in which God undertakes to purify, perfect, penetrate, and absorb the person in God. It is an encounter that is more delightful than all others.

Reflections on stanza one

This stanza describes the goal of contemplative life, union with God in love. This transformation in God is achieved by the Living Flame, who is the Holy Spirit. The stanza recognizes the abundance of God's love and gifts in the experience of spiritual marriage, it looks back to former times in the digression, and towards the end of the stanza it anxiously launches out to the goal of total union in eternity. A person who enters this experience feels on fire with the love of God and experiences in the depths of his or her being that he or she is enflamed with the love of God in union. This love of union is not acquired, it is given. The flame of love transforms and totally possesses the person so profoundly that he or she feels that there is no further goal in this life. This experience is a complete fusion of the activities of the person and the Holy Spirit. It is as if the person now experiences what John called "the what" of union with God.[15] The person feels the Holy Spirit in two ways—as a fire which consumes and transforms it, and as a fire that burns and flares up within it. So, there is a situation of transformation which is a permanent habit of life, and there are further moments, acts of love, when the Holy Spirit overwhelms the person's will with sublime love. The person now experiences union of wills, of hearts, of actions in conformity with God's, and of service and love of others. At this time the involvement of the Holy Spirit is so powerful that the person no longer acts on his or her own. Rather the Holy Spirit takes over the person's acts, making them God's acts. The Holy Spirit moves the soul in all its actions—however they are still the person's actions, for the Holy Spirit moves the person to do them. This experience is so transforming for anyone, "it makes the soul live in God spiritually and experience the life of God" (F. 1.6). This enjoyment of God in a living way is a foretaste of eternity.

The Holy Spirit, present as a Living Flame, touches the person with such profound love it seems like a burning wound caused by the tenderness of God. The person overwhelmed by this love dissolves and is absorbed in divine love. A person realizes that in these communications, God does everything and the person does nothing. All one can do now is to receive from God, to present no obstacle to God's work within, to consent and will only what God wills.

John's use of the term "flame of love" is very appropriate and is readily understood in the vocabulary of lovers. The flame of love refers to the intensity of feeling one has deep within one's heart. This burning love can be for a person, or for a mission, or for a common project or agenda. We have all felt this for someone we love; in fact we often refer to a person's lover as "a flame" because of the love given and the response of love that is generated. This description of the Holy Spirit is extraordinary both for the awesome transformation it implies and also for the depth of interaction with humanity.

The Living Flame's transformation takes place in the deepest center of a person, where one dwells with God, loving and enjoying God with his or her entire being and with every act, work, and inclination. The person is now motivated by the will of God in everything. When love permeates every aspect of a person's life, strength, and power, he or she can enter into God and center life on God alone. The stronger the love, the deeper will be the union. The more a person is transformed and concentrated in God the more intense, tender, stronger, and substantial is a person's delight. Granting these extraordinary blessings is part of the strategy of a generous and loving God who wants to dwell in anyone who has prepared for these gifts. "The Blessed Trinity inhabits the soul by divinely illumining its intellect with the wisdom of the Son, delighting its will in the Holy Spirit, and by absorbing it powerfully and mightily in the delightful embrace of the Father's sweetness" (F. 1. 15). There are two kinds of union that the Living Flame bestows on a person—union of love alone as an habitual presence, and union with an inflaming of love, when the intensity of love bursts forth, overwhelming the person with a vision of love and peace.

John describes this experience as "spiritual marriage." Several religious traditions have used marriage to describe the profound union of believers with God, no one more than Teresa of Avila and John of the Cross. John says: "This spiritual marriage is incomparably greater than the spiritual betrothal, for it is a total transformation in the Beloved, in which each surrenders the entire possession of self to the other with a certain consummation of the union of love" (C. 22.3). In marriage, two people give themselves to each other in an exclusive way. No one else matters in the same way. They express their love in any and every way they can. They are now on each other's side like never before, they trust each other unconditionally, they know they can rely on each other, they are now always there for each other. They gradually develop an integrated union that is intellectual, emotional, and physical. They are thrilled to be in each other's presence in big occasions and small occasions.

At this point in the *Living Flame* a person longs for the consummation of spiritual marriage. Although conformed to the will of God and transformed by love, a person still feels empty and lives in hope for the total completion of love that still lies ahead. This longing is no longer painful; it is love that longs for deeper love. Now, "love is the friend of the power of love" (F. 1.33). Having broken through the temporal veil of attraction to creatures, and the natural veil of inclinations and actions—both resulting from renunciation and purification, the person now wants to break through the third veil, the sensitive one that keeps him or her bound to this life. At this point, as the person longs for death, he or she thinks and wants what God thinks and wants, feels overwhelmed with the gifts and blessings received from God, and is ready to pass beyond the last veil. "God permits it in this state to discern its beauty and He entrusts to it the gifts and virtues he has bestowed, for everything is converted into love and praises" (F. 1. 31). A person at this point perceives the power of the next life, views everything as God does: "All things are nothing to it, and it is nothing in its own eyes; God alone is its all" (F. 1.32). The force of love that the person feels at this time makes him or her want to suffer no further delay in passing beyond this final veil of life. Having given oneself to love in this life, the person is ready for the final encounter.

Key concepts

"There is no reason to marvel at God granting such sublime and strange gifts" (F. Prologue .2).

Many people who read and study John of the Cross can readily identify with the challenges and struggles he describes in climbing Mount Carmel. They can see their own dark experiences in his descriptions of the dark night of the soul. They can also identify with the longings for love and union in the encounter of the lovers in the *Spiritual Canticle*. Yet, many of these devotees of John of the Cross do not find themselves in the *Living Flame of Love*. It is simply not for them—so they think. They know it describes the final stage of the spiritual life and are convinced few ever get there and feel their time and energy are best spent on the struggles of the journey. However, there is something about the *Living Flame* that helps put everything else into focus and makes everything else worthwhile. John tells us what it is—get used to God's generosity to us all.

The *Living Flame* describes how the Holy Spirit makes a person live in God. This transformation in the depths of one's personality is an encounter with the mystery of God that gives one a new source of identity and destiny. In this poem and commentary, the person is on fire with love, inflamed in divine union, immersed in the revelations of the Trinity, and so gifted that only a veil separates him or her from complete union. Of course, no one earns this. It is God who draws us to divine life, for God always takes the initiative, being the primary Lover. It is the nature of God to be love and to love. Always moved by infinite love, it is of the essence of God to extend love—it is who God is. Salvation history describes God's strategy of love for us all, and it tells us how God constantly takes a risk with us, sharing and inviting us to love.

Moreover God's gifts of love are not just for a small elite group. John reminds us that God "is not closefisted but diffuses Himself abundantly, as the sun does its rays, without being a respecter of persons" (F. 1.15). But, this is where John wants his readers to be real in appreciating God's awesome gifts of love, and so he insists, "There is no need to marvel at God granting such sublime and strange gifts" (F. Prologue.2). "Do not wonder that God brings some souls to this high peak" (F. 2. 5). Really, "There is no need to be amazed" (F. 2.36). John wants his readers to get used to God acting in this way.

John reminds us that God would want everyone at this level of life and union described in the *Living Flame*. He challenges us to appreciate that one's total life is involved in a union of love. In fact, every act is now love (C. 28.8). Nothing really matters anymore except to be in the union with a person we love with all our hearts. That union will be on all levels of life, and everything that is done is done for love. However, he finds few who are ready to make the commitment, and others who do not want to be guided to this goal (F. 2.27). He seems saddened to acknowledge that some do not relish the communications of God (F. 1.6), others just do not understand these gifts and find them incredible (F. 1.15), and still others do not have the basic experience needed to appreciate these profound challenges (F. 3.1). However, John insists that God grants these favors and does so according to the divine will. Generally, these gifts are made to those who "have performed many services for Him, have had admirable patience and constancy for His sake, and in their life and works have been very acceptable to Him" (F. 2.28). God purifies such people in varying degrees according to God's desire to raise them (F. 1.24), and leads them eventually to the remarkable delight of God's awakening (F. 4.5).

So, John reminds us not to be amazed that God grants such gifts. He reminds us twice (F. Prologue.2; 1.15) that Jesus told us that the Trinity would abide within anyone who loved

God. God is faithful to the divine nature and to these promises made. Put simply, God delights in giving and enriching those who seek divine union. God is seeking union in love with us more intensely than we seek it with God. We must look at the gifts we have received, marvel in God's love, and be aware of God's constant generosity towards us. We need to live with awareness that all life is a wonderful manifestation of God's love (see C. 24; 40). We must awaken ourselves to an appreciation of the reality that we are immersed in God's love. This changes the motivation for all our activities and gives us a new consciousness of the meaning of life. This is what the *Living Flame* calls us to appreciate and never to be amazed at this authentic vision of life. This is the new state of existence to which God calls all human beings.

Unfortunately, one of the great contemporary problems we face is indifference to the life of the spirit, as we immerse ourselves in the superficiality of religious devotions, thinking we can earn growth. In one of his sayings John urges us to keep things in perspective. "Who can free themselves from lowly manners and limitations if you do not lift them to yourself, my God, in purity and love? How will human beings begotten and nurtured in lowliness rise up to you, Lord, if you do not raise them with your hand that made them?" (S. 26). Aware of our own emptiness, the *Living Flame* reminds us that we grow primarily by receiving and cherishing the gifts of God. These gifts are not little supports here and there on our journey to God. They transform us into who we are intended to be. So, we need to think about life in light of the *Living Flame*; this is our goal, this is God's hope for us.

The Living Flame of love enflames the soul in strong, unitive love (see F. 1.1).

The *Living Flame* describes four aspects of the final stage in spiritual life, spiritual marriage, which John presented in the *Spiritual Canticle* (stanzas 22-35). To attain this fullness of union, John's doctrine is clear—nada, nothing. The *Ascent* and the *Dark Night* purify in view of a union of love. They describe a transformation that takes place in contemplation when we become receptive to God's activity within us, when God purifies our false desires, false loves, and false gods and fills us with an inflow of God's love. One's capacity for this love depends on the exclusive and integrated focus of every aspect of one's life. Prior to spiritual marriage the bride already evidenced love and surrender to her Bridegroom (C. 22.5), "but a singular fortitude and a very sublime love are also needed for so strong and intimate embrace from God" (C. 20-21.1). The *Spiritual Canticle* describes how the bride makes a complete surrender of herself to love, how she is "dissolved" in "such supreme and generous love" (C. 27.2). This loving union transforms a person and unites his or her will to God. This is a time of mutual surrender, profound communication, and total dedicated devotion to God's service (C. 28.3). The bride declares "All the ability of my soul and body . . . move in love and because of love. Everything I do I do with love, and everything I suffer I suffer with the delight of love" (C. 28.8). Towards the end of his description of spiritual marriage in the *Spiritual Canticle* John tells us how God values the bride's love because it is strong, and he adds, "this is why he loved her so much, he saw that her love was strong. . . alone and without other loves" (C. 31.5). A major change has taken place in this communion of love, "God here is the principal lover, who in the omnipotence of his fathomless love absorbs the soul in himself" (C. 31.2). From now on the bride's love will be God's loving in her, "so firmly united with the strength of God's will, with which he loves her, that her love for him is as strong and perfect as his love for her" (C. 38.3).

What the *Living Flame* makes clear is that this transformation in love in the very depths of a person is the work of the Holy Spirit, who wounds the soul with the tender love of God. John uses the term "wound of love" often, especially in the *Spiritual Canticle*. Generally, it describes the pain the bride experiences in her unfulfilled longings to be with her Lover. We all experience profound pain at the absence of someone we love intensely, a spouse, friend, parent, child, and so on. It is the empty space in our hearts that should be filled but is now empty. We feel the pain even more when we think about our loss. Sometimes this wound of love results from partial presence which instead of satisfying us leaves us in greater pain at a sense of absence and increases desire to be with someone. The more we experience and reflect on these partial presences the more we feel wounded with love.

The Holy Spirit fills the person with strong and unitive love in two ways: as a permanent presence, a habit of love, and as an enflaming of love in intense acts. As a person is thus transformed, all his or her actions cease to be his or her own for it is the Holy Spirit who now makes them and moves the person to union with God. These acts of love perfect a person in a short time, fortifying him or her in love (F. 1.33). John Welch explains this beautifully. "[W]hen the human spirit is transformed in a deep union of love with the Holy Spirit, motivation for our love shifts. The motivation for our love is no longer in us but now is in God. We now love but essentially do not have the reason for our love. The intention for our love has now moved, so to speak, into God. We love without knowing why; we simply love, and can do nothing but love. In our love, God is loving God and God's world. '. . . The soul here loves God, not through itself but through Him.'"[16] John tells us that a person feels this love in the very substance of his or her soul, in the deepest center of the human spirit. It is this stronger love and more unitive love that leads the person to God. "[L]ove is the soul's inclination, strength, and power in making its way to God, for love unites it with God. The more degrees of love it has, the more deeply it enters into God and centers itself in Him" (F. 1.13).

The *Living Flame* challenges us to think about human existence in a different way. Life and growth is what God is doing in us. God desires to share divine life with us, to communicate a new way of living and loving, and to establish an intimate relationship with each of us. We are called to live the life of God. If we can only remove obstacles to God's actions within us, then God is free to transform us into who we are intended to be, created to be. The psalmist reminds us that this steadfast love of God is precious, it is better than any other aspect of life (Ps 63.3). This transforming love of the Holy Spirit in this living flame gladdens a person's heart and allows him or her to enjoy "the glory of God's glory in likeness and shadow" (F. 3.16). The person possesses God in love and is possessed by God's love.

CHAPTER SIX

IMMERSED IN THE LIFE AND LOVE OF THE HOLY TRINITY (Stanza 2)

Overview of the stanza

T he second stanza of the poem proclaims that it is the Holy Trinity who effects the divine work of union. The Holy Spirit is a powerful fire of infinite love that transforms a person into itself. The gentle hand refers to the Father, generous and powerful, always ready to bestow gifts on the person. The only begotten Son of the Father is the delicate touch that wounds and cauterizes to bring this healing love.

> O sweet cautery,
>
> O delightful wound!
>
> O gentle hand! O delicate touch
>
> That tastes of eternal life

And pays every debt!

In killing You changed death to life.

The Holy Spirit working in a person purifies and enflames him or her according to the divine will and to each one's preparations. The Holy Spirit's communications of love are very strong and enflame the person in such a way that he or she becomes a burning fire for others. While this flame of love purifies, it does not consume, destroy, or afflict the person. Rather, it divinizes, and delights, as it burns gently. People who receive this communication find delight and satisfaction in its affliction. This experience is truly a contemplative communication of the divinity, who heals by wounding with love. So, this Flame of Love strengthens, empowers, and imbues a person with love. Since the burning wound is so wonderful, the person realizes how wonderful too must be the one who causes it.

The gentle and loving hand of the Father touches the person, wounding but bringing life and healing. When a person is refined, cleansed, purified, and withdrawn from every creature, he or she is ready to receive the Word, the Son of the Father, immense and delicate. The more abundantly the delicate touch pervades the person the purer he or she becomes. The delicate communication is indescribable, without form or figure, and simple. It is produced in the person by the simple infinite being of God who touches subtly, lovingly, eminently, and delicately. This touch is not yet perfect but anticipates eternal life. Sometimes, this experience of the touch of the Holy Spirit overflows to the body and sensory part. Thus, the body through this unction or anointing participates in the delights of the soul.

[There follows a digression, F. 2.23-31].

There are two kinds of life. The first consists in the vision of God attained by natural death. The second is perfect spiritual life acquired through purification, for without mortification one cannot attain the perfection of the spiritual life of union with God. In the new life, faculties (intellect, will, and memory) are focused on God and appetites and activities become divine. The soul thus transformed lives the life of God—it has changed from death to spiritual life. The intellect becomes one with God's intellect. God's will and a person's will are now one. The memory no longer perceives the figures of creatures but is united to the mind and future of God. Natural appetites that used to relish creatures now find fulfillment in God alone. All movements and operations of the person are now dead to their former life and alive to God and moved by the Holy Spirit. So the person becomes God through participation—dead to all he or she used to be and alive to what God is.

Reflections on stanza two

Part of the experience of spiritual marriage is the transforming work of the Holy Trinity indwelling in the person who reaches this state. This experience is of all three working together as one, and yet it seems to the person that each one of the Trinity has a particular role to play. The Holy Spirit cauterizes the person with a delightful wound. The Son shares a delicate touch that gives a taste of eternal life. The Father transforms the person with a gentle hand that pays all former debts. This transformation is the efficacious gift of the Trinity and the person looks with gratitude at both the gift and the Giver.

The Holy Spirit transforms a person by touching him or her with the fire of love that is so intense it cauterizes the soul, burning away imperfections and transforming the person into a burning flame. When we use the term "cautery" we mean a burning, generally of the skin, and the doctor does this to stop the bleeding, to purify the wound and prevent infection, and to begin the healing process. It seems terrible at the time but is later appreciated as the one great healing that gave one chance for a new life. We use the term here to imply the stopping of the hemorrhaging of the spiritual life. Here in the poem the cauterizing flame does not consume or destroy or afflict, but divinizes and delights the person. The flame does not weary or restrict the person but enlarges, and enriches him or her. Other effects of this cauterizing include communications, personal satisfaction, and fulfillment. This cauterizing causes a delightful wound of love. When someone receives a burn he or she needs medicine to cure it, but this burning is the medicine; the more it wounds the more it cures and heals. "The more wounded the lover, the healthier he is, and the cure love causes is to wound . . . to such an extent that the entire soul is dissolved into a wound of love" (F. 2.7). Thus the person becomes healthy in love and transformed in love. The Holy Spirit produces this cauterizing activity in order to bring delight to the person according to the capacity of each one.

The flame of love of which we speak is a touch of the divinity in the person without any intellectual form or figure. We all appreciate that touching someone can have a healing affect and healthcare workers often tell us to touch a patient to show our compassionate presence. But touching is also a sign of affection, as when grandparents caress their grandchildren. Touch is also a form of romance for lovers who both feel thrilled at their closeness and exclusive relationship. This experience of the touch of God fills stanza two. Not only does John mention it many times, but he also directly addresses the touch personally five times; "O you then, delicate touch" (F. 2.17-21). There are other experiences of the burning and transforming action of God in the person, which spiritual people have described to us. "Nevertheless, when the wound is made only in the soul without being communicated outwardly, the delight can be more intense and sublime" (F. 2. 13). One does not attain the peak experiences of the wound of love without leaving aside activity of the senses. However, the effects of the spirit can overflow to the senses; they then proceed from inner strength and appear outwardly as energy, peace, and well-being.

The merciful and omnipotent Father treats each one with a gentle hand. Human beings express themselves through their bodies and the gentle hand can heal, calm, console, encourage, sympathize, and support. It is very special that John sees the Father treating us in this way. Although nations tremble before the power of God, God treats each one with extraordinary gentleness. "You are friendly and gentle with me, how much more lovingly, graciously, and gently do You permanently touch my soul!" (F. 2.16). This gentle hand causes death and gives life. "You have wounded me in order to cure me, O divine hand, and you have put to death in me what made me lifeless, deprived me of God's life in which I now see myself live" (F. 2.16).

The delicate touch is brought to the person by the Word, the Son of God, who penetrates a person's very substance transforming him or her in God. Although terrible and strong, the Son touches a person with gentleness when he is permanently hidden within a person who is refined, cleansed, and purified. Thus, the Son withdraws the person from all other interests to focus on himself alone, pervading the person's very substance. "O Word, indescribably delicate touch, produced in the soul only by Your most simple being, which, since it is infinite, is infinitely delicate and hence touches so subtly, lovingly, eminently, and delicately!" (F. 2.20). This touch is so special that it gives a taste of eternal life, as inexpressibly profound as is possible in this life. "As a result the soul tastes here all the things of God, since God communicates to it fortitude, wisdom, love, beauty, grace, and goodness, etc. Because God is all these things, a person enjoys them in only one touch of God, and the soul rejoices within its faculties and within its substance" (F. 2.21). This experience can be so deep that it overflows into the body that then shares in these delights.

John's mysticism is eminently Trinitarian. This is his distinctive way of speaking about God and of explaining our participation in divine life. While John's focus on the Trinity permeates the entire poem and commentary, it is particularly pronounced in stanza two. The Holy Trinity acting as one changes death into life. There are two kinds of life; that which comes after death and consists in the vision of God, and that which comes from purification that leads to the possession of God in the union of love. In this latter case, a person brings death to the old life, and through union with God he or she lives the life of God. A person has passed from death to a new spiritual life. This happens when the intellect is moved and formed by faith, the will changed into a life of divine love, the memory changed into possession of God in a vision of hope, and the appetites changed so that they now delight in God alone. Every aspect of one's being is now alive to God. "Accordingly, the intellect of this soul is God's intellect; its will is God's will; its memory is the memory of God; its delight is God's delight" (F. 2.34). The person has now become God through participation. He or she is dead to former life and alive to God who continually renews all things. The person rejoices in this new life, grateful to God who has wrought this transformation by changing death into life.

Key concepts

The Holy Trinity, always solicitous, changes death to life (see F. 2.1).

John of the Cross has a wonderful grasp of the spiritual life and balances ordinary everyday values with insights into the most extraordinary communications of divine life. John's entire system centers on God whom he sees as the principal agent in spiritual life, drawing people to divine life and taking the initiative at every stage. God's love precedes all human response, purifying, illuminating, supporting, sharing, transforming, and intervening in extraordinary ways. All this takes place against a backdrop of four key basic qualities of God. First, God is master of divine self-communication and gifts, bestowing blessings on people no matter their readiness. "For God grants them to whom he wills and for the reason he wills" (A. 2. 32.2). Men and women can do nothing except respect God's sovereign will, for we do not understand God's ways. When God grants special graces, men and women can only stand by in wonder, for "there is no reason, or possibility of a reason, why God should look at and exalt her, but that this reason is only in God" (C. 33.2). The second basic quality of God is that God loves and gives without measure, spreading gifts with loving liberality (C. 27.1), for God is "as generous and bountiful as [he] is powerful and rich" (F. 2.16). So, along these lines, God participates in mutual surrender, self-gift, and loving union. The third basic quality that John sees in God is that love leads God to adapt to each person's unique situation, like a loving parent adapting to the needs of each child, even condescending to treat some for a time according to their own desires (A.2. 21.3). However, this special, personal love of God eventually draws a person away from his or her childish behavior and leads to deeper union. The fourth basic quality of God that John considers important as background for spiritual development is that God works through the normal sacramental economy of the Church. Thus, he warns followers away from the exceptional, preternatural gifts, and urges dedication to the basic plan of God (see A.2. 22.15 and A.3. 31.9).

These four basic concepts form the solid theological and ecclesiological backdrop for John's vision of God's interventions in our lives. However, with the *Living Flame* something happens that overwhelms all else. We discover that God's solicitousness, seen in the four basic foundational qualities, is intensified, as God renews a person's entire life in transforming love, bringing him or her to new experiences never anticipated. "You are friendly and gentle with me; how much more lovingly, generously, and gently do you permanently touch my soul" (F. 2.16). The Trinity—sweet cautery, delightful wound, and delicate hand—cures and heals as it cauterizes, transforms a person into itself as it touches, and gives a taste of eternal life as it communicates to the soul. Thus, a person can say, "The more it wounds, the more it cures and heals" (F. 2.7).

The second stanza of the *Living Flame* emphasizes how the Trinity transforms into itself the person it touches, changing every aspect of death into life. Thus John comments on God's action within a person; "you cause death and you give life" (F. 2.16), and "you put to death in me what made me lifeless" (F. 2.16). The whole of the spiritual journey is a movement from death to life; in fact, God uses death to gain life. The first step is, "You detach and withdraw the soul from all other touches of created things by the might of your delicacy. . . so mild an effect you leave in the soul" (F. 2.18). Then God grants favors to the person, exalting, enlarging, and delighting him or her with gifts that act like the mustard seed and spread and grow. In the *Living Flame*, God takes up abode in the person's heart; "He takes up His abode in a man by making him live the life of God and dwell in the Father, the Son, and the Holy Spirit" (F. Prologue.2). When this happens, a person feels God's presence within like a burning fire. In fact, the person feels "transformed into a flame of love, in which the Father, the Son, and the Holy Spirit are communicated to it" (F. 1.6). In this way the flame changes death to life and "makes the soul live in God spiritually and experience the life of God" (F. 1.6). Thus, the flame makes a person live God's life, eternal life, by communicating the tenderness of God's life and by granting profound love.

The death that the Trinity brings about concerns old ways of thinking, possessing, and loving. "Let it be known that what the soul calls death is all that goes to make up the old man: the entire engagement of the faculties (memory, intellect, and will) in the things of the world. . . . All this is the activity of the old life, which is death to the new life of the spirit" (F. 2.33). However, the indwelling of the Holy Trinity transforms the three great spiritual faculties. "The Blessed Trinity inhabits the soul by divinely illuminating its intellect with the wisdom of the Son, delighting its will in the Holy Spirit, and by absorbing it powerfully and mightily in the unfathomed embrace of the Father's sweetness" (F. 1.15). It is interesting that John uses this term, for sweetness refers to the wonderful qualities of the giver and contrasts with its opposite "bitterness." When someone treats us with bitterness we immediately feel like rejecting them, whereas gentleness and sweetness gains our full attention, welcome, appreciation, and joy. Someone who treats us with sweetness makes us feel loved and appreciated. We know they want what is best for us. This is the Father's approach to us.

John says the Trinity achieves this by acting in the strength of love as a cautery, a delicate touch, and a gentle hand—all changing death to life (F. 2.1). In this way the Trinity converts a person into a fire of love. Of this transformation each person can say, "You have put to death in me what made me lifeless, deprived me of God's life in which I now see myself live. You granted this with the liberality of your generous grace" (F. 2.16). The *Living Flame* tells us how all this is done by the Trinity's transforming love. John quotes an interesting verse from the prophet Hosea: "O death, I will be your death" (Hosea 13.14). Thus, God absorbs the person in life.

Finding satisfaction in God alone (see F. 2.21).

Sooner or later, human beings must arrive at the awareness that they can never be fulfilled except in union with God. From the earliest times of his life, John of the Cross was deeply aware of this. "I no longer live within myself and I cannot live without God, for having neither him nor myself what will life be? It will be a thousand deaths, longing for my true life and dying because I do not die" (Stanzas of the soul that suffers with longing to see God, 1). This is not a confession of faith by John but an experience, a deep awareness of the reality of life and God. In one of John's extraordinarily beautiful sayings, "The prayer of a soul taken with love," he gives insight into his understanding of finding satisfaction in God alone. This saying, which some writers consider autobiographical, develops in a continuing crescendo from the misery of sin to humble abandonment, to confidence in Jesus, and finally to the enthusiastic possession of everything in the Lord. It is not that John possesses God alone, but that he possesses everything in God. This is not the result of detachment but of a vision of total spiritual integration. "Mine are the heavens and mine is the earth. Mine are the nations, the just are mine, and mine the sinners. The angels are mine, the Mother of God, and all things are mine; and God Himself is mine and for me, because Christ is mine and all for me" (S. 27). So, John concludes with a warning to us; do not take crumbs that fall from the table, rather find satisfaction in a totally God directed life that includes everything.

In spiritual marriage a person finds satisfaction in God alone. This includes mutual knowledge and union in love in which the two natures become one spirit. This mutual surrender, equality in love, means total mutual sharing where each keeps back nothing. Finding satisfaction in each other brings peace and the mutual enkindling of deeper mature love. This love is based on deeper knowledge, an intimate sharing of each one's deepest hopes and longings. It implies that a person uses all his or her faculties and possessions in this total commitment. Such a person loves God in everything and has no other interests except in the pursuit of the practice of love. At this time one understands that there is no greater or more necessary work than love and so he or she is constantly attentive to love in all he or she does with no concern for anything else. Rather, a person loses interest in everything else. As John says in the *Spiritual Canticle*, "He who truly walks in love lets himself lose all things immediately in order to be found more attached to what he loves" (C. 29.10). The result of this pursuit of God alone is that God gives the impression of finding satisfaction in one who seeks union (C. 32.6). Then, they just like to spend time in each other's company. "Strange it is, this property of lovers, that they like to enjoy one another's companionship alone, apart from every creature and all company" (C. 36.1).

Finding satisfaction in God alone means desiring only what God desires, loving as God loves, and seeking mutuality in every aspect of life. It means total faithfulness, conforming one's will to God's in self-gift and obedience, accepting everything that comes from the will of God. It means redirecting ones spiritual faculties to focus on God alone; knowing, loving, and possessing God in a new way. Then a person can say, "What you desire me to ask for, I ask for; and what you do not desire, I do not desire, nor can I, nor does it even enter my mind to desire it" (F. 1.36). In fact, the Trinity takes over the actions of a person, so that all his or her operations are now divine.

The *Living Flame* reminds us that human fulfillment is found in God alone at every stage in the journey, but more so in the final experience of union. Until this final experience the person "still lives in hope, in which one cannot fail to feel emptiness" (F. 1.27). When the Trinity bestows transforming love a person catches a glimpse—as if through a thin veil—of the total union that lies beyond. A person's longing to find satisfaction in God alone arrives at a place where "All things are nothing to it, and it is nothing in its own eyes; God alone is its all" (F. 1.32). While a person can only give what it has been given, "A reciprocal love is thus actually formed between God and the soul, like the marriage union and surrender, in which the goods of both . . . are possessed by both together" (F. 3.79). Thus, a person finds its satisfaction in God alone.

The *Living Flame* emphasizes the spiritual reality that finding satisfaction in God alone is a gift. A person contributes but even the little he or she does is because God has bestowed these desires on the person. The pursuit of satisfaction in mutual surrender is the Trinity's work within us. The living God desires to abide in us and communicate divine life to us. We seek to possess God but find we are possessed by God; we seek to love and find we are loved totally by God; we seek union and realize it is a gift. It is the purifying cautery of the Holy Spirit that wounds with love, the delicate touch of the Son that gives a taste of eternal life, and the gentle hand of the Father that brings about this transformation. Together and individually the Trinity achieves the purpose of exalting, enlarging, and delighting a person in such a way that he or she finds satisfaction in God alone.

CHAPTER SEVEN

TRANSFORMED BY GOD'S LOVE AND ATTRIBUTES (Stanza 3)

Overview of the stanza

This third stanza of the poem describes how a person is immersed in the life and love of the Holy Trinity. God discloses the divine life to a person in descriptors or attributes which become like lamps giving light and heat to the person. God is all these attributes in simple oneness of being, and the person experiences these attributes in one simple act of union.

O lamps of fire!

In whose splendors

The deep caverns of feeling,

Once obscure and blind,

Now give forth, so rarely, so exquisitely,

Both warmth and light to their Beloved.

God reveals the divine self to a person by means of the divine attributes. These become like many lamps in the person, each one distinctly and all of them together giving knowledge and enflaming him or her in love. God's omnipotence becomes a lamp of omnipotence, sharing and bestowing all knowledge. God as wisdom becomes a lamp of wisdom in the person. Likewise, the divine attributes of goodness, justice, fortitude, mercy, and all others, communicate light and envelop the person in love, so he or she experiences all these attributes vitally. The person delights in this experience, as each lamp burns in love and enlightens and enflames all the other lamps. Thus, the person enjoys all attributes together, and each one separately but always enriched by all the others. Absorbed in the love of these attributes, a person becomes more alive in love and perceives that love is the essential aspect of eternal life. A person experiences that God is wise and loves with wisdom, is infinitely good and loves with goodness, is holy and with holiness loves. So, God loves the person with the full power of all the divine attributes—loving with justice, mercy, liberality, absolute humility, and so on. In this way God reveals and communicates the divine self in this union, while a person is transformed through participation in God and in God's attributes.

Each of God's attributes gives forth loving knowledge to the person, transforming him or her into each of these attributes. This transformation takes place through the interaction of the person and the Holy Spirit. These vital divine revelations can also be called "overshadowings" for through them God casts a shadow of protection over the person. Thus, the shadow of God's beauty cast over the person will be another beauty based on God's beauty, of God's fortitude another fortitude, of God's wisdom another wisdom, and so on with the other attributes or lamps. Since a person cannot comprehend God fully in this life, he or she will always experience a shadow of God's beauty, wisdom, fortitude, and so on. However, a person will recognize that the shadow cast is clearly God's shadow. The divine attributes are simple being and are enjoyed distinctly, and yet each one enkindles the others, and each is substantially the others. Each one is known and enjoyed so as not to hinder the perfect knowledge and enjoyment of the other. Yet, each one throws light on the others.

[There follows John's longest digression, F. 3.18-67, which is presented in chapter 2 and the second appendix to chapter 2].

In preparation for union with God in spiritual marriage God anoints the faculties—intellect, will, and memory—but the suffering that is part of the experience can be intense. Anointing means setting aside someone or something for a special purpose or function. So, we anoint kings, and priests, and even some of the symbols of their office. We want God to anoint our spiritual faculties so that our intellect, memory, and will are set aside to be focused exclusively on God and enable us to know, possess, and love God in an exclusive way. At that time the satisfaction, fullness, and delight of the faculties will be great when they are transformed by the possession of divine knowledge, love, and glory. Through his or her three faculties a person experiences and enjoys the objects of the spiritual faculties, the grandeurs of God's wisdom and excellence. Through these deep caverns of feeling (the faculties) a person has power and capacity for experiencing, possessing, and tasting the deep knowledge and splendors of the attributes of God.

Before God enlightens and illumines a person, he or she dwells in obscurity, and when in sin is blind, and even though God's light shines on him or her, he or she cannot see it. A person is blind in total darkness because of sin, but one can be in obscurity without sin. Before reaching union the person was in obscurity regarding natural and supernatural things. He or she naturally desired only darkness because of knowing what it was—going from darkness to darkness guided by darkness. The person was also blind when his or her appetites acted like a cataract, allowed to see only a little of the divine riches and beauty. Even a small appetite obstructs the clear vision of divine grandeurs. So, people who have not purified their appetites and faculties consider some base things as highly important and some things precious to the spirit as of little value. So, a person lived in obscurity without divine light, blind through its appetites and affections. Now with purified faculties a person has become filled with the brightness of God and resplendent.

When the faculties are pervaded with the illumination of the attributes, they give loving glory to God and surrender themselves to God, reflecting back the light they have received. The intellect receives divine wisdom exquisitely, and returns it to God in the same excellence. It also receives goodness in excellence and returns it in excellence. So, according to the excellence of the divine attributes that the Beloved communicates, corresponds the excellence with which a person gives back. In union a person is now God through participation—sharing in God's qualities. As God gave self totally, so he or she gives self totally to God. In this way a person can offer to God the gift of the Holy Spirit, as if this gift were his or her own. Thus, a person gives to God all that God freely gave and thereby repays love with a suitable gift. God accepts this gift gratefully, as if the person were giving something of himself or herself—even greater than self. Thus, God re-surrenders to the person, and the person loves God as if again. This reciprocal love is like a spiritual marriage in which the goods of each are possessed by both. This wonderful transformation is not as perfect as in the next life.

A person enjoys fullness in the union of the intellect and affection with God and surrenders totally to God in wonderful ways. Concerning love, first, the person loves God not through himself or herself but through God, loving through the Holy Spirit as the Father and the Son love each other. Second, the person also loves God in God, for he or she is now absorbed in God. Third, the person loves God on account of who God is—not because God is generous or glorious, but because God is all this in essence. Regarding fruition and fullness, the person now enjoys God by means of God, since its intellect is now united to all the attributes of God. Second, he or she enjoys God directly without intermingling of creatures. Third the person enjoys God because of who God is in the divine self without seeking pleasure for itself. The person praises God excellently. First, seeing it as a duty, second, for the gifts received, and third because of who God is without any thought of benefit. The person expresses the excellence of gratitude: first for all natural and spiritual goods received, second because of finding great delight in praising God, and third, because of who God is.

Reflections on stanza three

The first stanza celebrates how the Holy Spirit transforms in the deepest center of being the person who reaches spiritual marriage. The second stanza proclaims that the experience of spiritual marriage is the transforming work of the Holy Trinity; the Holy Spirit cauterizes the person with a delightful wound, the Son shares a delicate touch that gives a taste of eternal life, and the Father transforms the person with a gentle hand that pays all former debts. This third stanza rejoices in the fact that the person receives abundant and lofty knowledge of God, communications of light and love to the three spiritual faculties of intellect, memory, and will. This communication is so illumined and filled with love that the person becomes a source of light and love for others. Appreciating these gifts, the person sings of this new transformed life he or she has received.

No one can know God fully in this life, but we try to appreciate the divine life by means of a series of descriptors or attributes. John suggests we participate in these attributes. When we admire someone's special gifts without jealousy we often want to imitate them, be like them, embody the qualities we appreciate so much. We would like to participate in the gifts and talents in which they excel. We want to be like them. This is the challenge here. We say that God is almighty, wise, good, merciful, just, powerful, and loving, and so on. "God in His unique and simple being is all the powers and grandeurs of His attributes" (F. 3.2). In the transformation described in this stanza, God communicates this knowledge to the person—that God is each of these qualities distinctly and all of them together in simple oneness of being. This communication is so transformative for the person, that he or she becomes these attributes in union with God. "We deduce that the soul, like God, gives forth light and warmth through each of these innumerable attributes. Each of these attributes is a lamp which enlightens it and transmits the warmth of love" (F. 3. 2). John calls each of these attributes a lamp of fire because lamps give both light and heat, and each of these attributes of God gives illumination and love to the person. Thus, when God communicates divine omnipotence to the soul, the soul knows that omnipotence and love go together. When God communicates wisdom, God "grants the soul light and the warmth of the love of God according to His wisdom" (F. 3.3). Likewise God communicates all the other divine attributes. This is not simply intellectual knowledge of God but living, vivifying, and vital knowledge. The person does not just know this about God but experiences it. Moreover, the person's experience is not just of each one separately but of all together at the same time, each one influencing all the others. "Each lamp burns in love, and the warmth from each furthers the warmth of the other, and the flame of one, the flame of the other, just as the light of one sheds light on the other, because through each attribute the other is known" (F. 3.5). The communication of the vital interrelationship of all these attributes is wonderful. They are not just illuminating but loving, and "the soul perceives clearly that love is proper to eternal life" (F. 3.5).

Each one loves and does good according to his or her nature. God loves us with omnipotence, wisdom, mercy, justice, and so on; God loves with the full force of all the divine attributes. God is omnipotent and loves us omnipotently, God is holy and loves with holiness, God is truth and loves with truthfulness, and so on. God's communications are like lamps of fire, bringing light and warmth. They are also like living waters of the spirit that refresh and satisfy thirst. John concludes this section; "Everything can be expressed in this statement: The soul becomes God from God through participation in Him and in His attributes, which it terms the 'lamps of fire'" (F. 3.8).

These lamps of fire are not like other lamps that give light and warmth around them to people who are distinct from them. In these divine communications the person is absorbed within the attributes of God and transformed in them. So, a person's spiritual faculties are transformed because they are absorbed within the attributes of God, and the lamps of fire are constantly granting further gifts in order to lead the person to eternal life and deeper union.

John calls the divine attributes "lamps of fire", but he also thinks of them as "overshadowings," since they cast a shadow of protection, favor, and grace to the person. Each divine attribute casts a shadow of itself; divine wisdom casts a shadow of wisdom on the person, God's beauty casts a protective shadow of beauty over the person, God's infinite goodness casts a grace-filled goodness on the person, and so on. It is extraordinary to see the awesome generosity of God in the gifts bestowed on the person in this spiritual state described in the third stanza.

In this profound divine communication the spiritual faculties of intellect, memory, and will are transformed. John calls these faculties "the deep caverns of feeling" for it is through them that a person experiences and enjoys the revelation of divine communication in the attributes. Prior to God's enlightenment and illumination these faculties were "once obscure and blind." God illumines the faculties through the vital communication of divine attributes; this is entirely gift, something the faculties could never have attained on their own. Previously, the faculties responded like a person who has a cataract over they eye, never seeing things clearly, but rather pursuing objects they thought were important although they never were. Once the spiritual faculties have been illumined by communication of the divine attributes, they surrender to a new purpose—to give back the light and heat they have received. The intellect is now united to God's intellect, the will is united to God's goodness and gives back that same goodness to God. "And according to the excellence of the divine attributes (fortitude, beauty, justice, etc.), which the Beloved communicates, is the excellence with which the soul's feelings give joyfully to Him the very light and heat it receives from Him" (F. 3.78). Thus, the person in this state is one with God and God through participation—the intellect of the two is one intellect, the will of the two is one will, and the memory of the two is one vision of life, and God's operation and the person's is one.

A person at this point rejoices in being able to give back to God something of his or her own; "giving all that was given it by Him in order to repay love" (F. 3.79). This reciprocal gift of love and total mutual surrender is part of the spiritual marriage described in these stanzas. "This is the soul's deep satisfaction and happiness: to see that it gives to God more than in itself it is worth" (F. 3.80). The spiritual faculties are transformed and surrender themselves to God in renewed love, fulfillment, praise, and gratitude.

Key concepts

Experiencing God—perceiving love is essential to life (see F. 3.5).

After an initial period of purification in the *Spiritual Canticle*, the person who seeks God enters a phase of illumination and finds that in contemplation God begins to reveal divine life to each one. Knowledge of God up to this point was mediated through creatures, other people, even the spirit world. However, the bride of the poem says she has had enough of these messages, stammerings, and partial revelations. Rather, she wants to experience her Beloved face to face. "Do not send me any more messengers, they cannot tell me what I must hear" (C. stanza 6). "She asks him that from henceforth he no longer detain her with any other knowledge, communications, and traces of his excellence since, rather than bringing her satisfaction these increase her longings and suffering" (C. 6.2). John now speaks about "contemplative experience," and "living contemplation and knowledge." The bride asks for complete mutual surrender so that she might enjoy "essential knowledge," real knowledge that goes beyond other communications. The experience she seeks is a mystical revelation "which is known through love, and by which one not only knows but at the same time experiences" (C. Prologue.3). Experience and enjoyment is not mediated, it is immediate; it is not sense-based conceptual but spiritual; it is not something we actively engage in but passively enjoy. Yet it is the result of an interaction between God and the person. Religious experience results from an encounter between two realms of life—this present one and a realm of life beyond this one that gives meaning to this one. It seems that we touch something, or someone, beyond the normal horizons of life, and the experience gives us insight beyond all previous knowing. John says we feel or taste this experience (he uses the Spanish "se gustan"). Some experiences happen to us and we are glad when they are over and we want to forget them as soon as possible. We feel some other experiences are so good we want to taste and savor them in such a way that we can often relive them and remind ourselves of the impact they had on us. This experience beyond the normal horizons of life is very personal, and no one else can have this experience for us. In fact, we cannot even control it ourselves. It happens to us. We cannot earn this experience, we can only recognize it as a gift of God and receive it with gratitude. "This experience of God occurs within ordinary human experience. God is so intimate to the experience that God is not a third thing, so we do not have the self, a sunset, and then God. In the interactive experience of the self and the sunset God is co-experienced, co-present, co-known."[17] Thus, John can say, "My Beloved, the mountains, and lonely wooded valleys, strange islands. . ." (C. stanza 14).

The *Living Flame* deals with a person's very intimate and qualified union with and transformation in God, dealing as it does with matters that are interior, spiritual, and beyond sense. These favors are granted by God, and "The soul feels that it is all inflamed in divine union . . . in the most intimate part of its substance" (F. 1.1). John says that one feels God within, senses a flame burning within, has an intense desire, feels taken over by the Spirit. He describes experience as delighting, tasting, savoring, enjoying, and he speaks of God touching, wounding, and moving. "Thus in this flame the soul experiences God so vividly and tastes Him with such delight and sweetness that it exclaims: O living flame of love!" (F. 1.6). The experience of God takes place in a person's deepest center, in the very substance of the spirit, in that point of interiority within the human spirit. John suggests that in a sublime experience a person is conscious, knows full well, feels and understands what the Holy Spirit grants, as the Spirit deifies the person's substance. "This is a touch of substance, that is, of the substance of God in the substance of the soul" (F. 2.21). The experience is stronger the more substantially the transformation touches a person's inner spirit. John continually describes experience as something the person spiritually feels, senses, delights in, and enjoys.[18]

The *Living Flame* describes the goal and end of the spiritual journey. It describes the experience of a person who has journeyed to the center of his or her humanity and there discovered the revelation of God's love. In this life-giving experience one is no longer oneself as before but a new self transformed in God's love. In this encounter or experience of God a person knows, possesses, and loves God in new ways. John agrees with theologians and philosophers of the ages that we know God through the divine attributes. Each of these attributes reflects the divine self. "Each of these attributes is the very being of God in his one and only suppositum, which is the Father, the Son, and the Holy Spirit" (F. 3.2). When John speaks about experiencing God in contemplation, he says "God is the direct object of this knowledge in that one of his attributes (his omnipotence, fortitude, goodness, sweetness, and so on) is sublimely experienced" (A.2 26.3). However, this is not just knowledge or a statement of faith, rather a person experiences God's attributes vitally, encountering God as goodness, fortitude, mercy, compassion, and so on. A person enjoys God as goodness, fortitude, etc, and becomes aware that "God in his unique and simple being is all the power and grandeur of his attributes" (F. 3.2). In addition to the usual attributes of God John adds a special one, namely that he experiences God as beauty and he identifies this with the essence of God (C. 11.2). When a person is in union, God deigns to disclose knowledge of the divine attributes and this revelation fills the person with love. "Hence, the soul in one act of knowledge of these lamps (attributes) loves through each one and, in so doing, loves through them all together, bearing in that act the quality of love for each one and from each one, and from all together and for all together" (F. 3. 3). So, each attribute permeates all the others and gives the soul a multifaceted experience of God's love. John goes on to say that each of these attributes, lamps, splendors, conveys a loving experience of God to the soul, transforms the soul into each of these qualities of God, and overshadows the soul with the protection of the attribute. Experiencing these attributes vitally, a person enjoys them, delights in knowing God in them, and savors how they each enrich the others. The soul becomes these attributes and returns them in praise to God. According to stanza three of the *Living Flame*, we encounter God through an experiential knowing of the divine attributes—tasting, feeling, enjoying, delighting in knowing God in this way.

Transforming the spiritual faculties—experiencing divine transformation (see F. 3.68).

The spiritual journey to God is sometimes described as a journey of faith, or a journey of love, or the seeking of God through the nights to union. It is also possible to see the whole spiritual journey as the purification, redirection, and transformation of the spiritual faculties. People who dedicate themselves to God generally think they know God, possess God, and love God, but this knowledge, possession, and love is so far from authentic that it is damaging to one's pursuit of God. The intellect can accumulate knowledge, the memory can gather all its wonderful images, and the will can focus on its many loves, but together these do not correspond to God. The work of purifying these faculties begins in the active night of sense. "[T]he soul is not united with God in this life through understanding, or through enjoyment, or through imagination, or through any other sense; but only faith, hope and charity (according to the intellect, memory, and will) can unite the soul with God in this life" (A.2. 6.1). The intellect, memory, and will must turn away from their normal objects of knowledge, possessions, and loves to focus instead on faith, hope, and love. "At this stage a person suffers from sharp trials in his intellect, severe dryness and distress in his will, and from the burdensome knowledge of his own miseries in his memory" (F. 1.20). We know more about God in faith than in the accumulation of knowledge. We possess God more in hope than we do in memories. We love God more in charity than we do in accumulated desires. At first the three theological virtues cause emptiness and darkness in the faculties, leading a person to abandon all previous knowledge, possessions, and loves. "We must lead the faculties of the soul to these three virtues and inform each faculty with one of them by stripping and darkening it of everything which is not conformable to these virtues" (A.2. 6.6). The spiritual journey implies emptying ourselves of all that is not God, so we can attain what is truly of God.

In the large digression of stanza three in the *Living Flame* John considers how "The deep caverns of feeling, once obscure and blind, now give forth, so rarely, so exquisitely, both warmth and light to their Beloved." The "caverns of feeling" are the spiritual faculties that have been emptied of false knowledge in the intellect, false hopes in the memory, and false loves and desires in the will. They experience profound pain in their emptiness and can easily be tempted to fill the void with "Any little thing that adheres to them in this life" (F. 3.18). They are in pain because they long for God to fill them with authentic knowledge, hope, and love. "And this feeling that is so intense commonly occurs toward the end of illumination and purification, just before the attainment of union, where a person is then satisfied" (F. 3.18). With the union described in the *Living Flame* the pain of emptiness and longing gives way to satisfaction, fullness, and delight, as God transforms the spiritual faculties, filling them with divine communications through the revelation of the attributes. This is the transformation that takes place in spiritual marriage. "The soul here calls these three faculties (memory, intellect, and will) the deep caverns of feeling because through them and in them it deeply experiences and enjoys the grandeurs of God's wisdom and excellence" (F. 3.69). Now the pain of emptiness gives way to the joy of fulfillment, and one's intellect, memory, and will are now God's (see F. 2.34).

So, a person experiences God in the very substance of the soul, where he or she feels transformed and gifted with new knowledge in faith, possession in hope, and love in charity. The spiritual faculties are now illuminated from the inside, rather than as formerly from the outside. Now a person can give to God a genuine appreciation of who God is, returning to God what he or she has received. So, now the intellect receives the divine wisdom, being made one with God's intellect, the will is united to goodness and loves as God loves, and the memory is transformed in hope. The person now knows, loves, and hopes, having experienced vitally the divine attributes. In his or her deepest regions of inner spirit a person is transformed in God. The whole journey of the spiritual life consists in this transformation of the spiritual faculties. In this transformation a person learns new ways of knowing, hoping, and loving God. This is a passive experience in which God is the teacher and guide. It is the time when a person becomes his or her true self by identifying totally with God's revelation.

CHAPTER EIGHT

UNDERSTANDING THE COSMOS IN UNION WITH THE LOVE OF THE WORD (Stanza 4)

Overview of the stanza

This final stanza of the Living Flame of Love describes how a person gains an understanding of the whole cosmos in union with the love of the Word. The Lord of the world united to the entire cosmos graces the person with love.

> How gently and lovingly
>
> You wake in my heart,
>
> Where in secret You dwell alone;
>
> And in Your sweet breathing,

Filled with good and glory,

How tenderly You swell my heart with love.

The person in search of divine union here addresses God with deep love, thanking God for the effects produced from this union, namely an awakening of the person's spirit in gentleness and love and the breathing of God in the person. So, the person experiences an awakening of love in the very center and depths of his or her being, and feels so captivated and aroused in love that it seems the whole world participates in this intense movement of love. In this experience a person sees the beauty of everything in the world, and he or she appreciates how all creatures find their life and strength in God. Here is the delight of this awakening: a person knows creatures through God and not God through creatures. God reveals to the person the divine life and being and the harmony of every creature in that divine life. So, a person sees God in essence and God in relationship to all the creatures of the world. Through this cosmic awakening, a person sees God and God in creation at least partially.

What a person knows and experiences of God in this awakening is beyond words. It is the communication of God's excellence to a person's inner substance. This awesome revelation is one of terrible and solid array of divine power, but a person is made gentle and charming with all the gentleness and charm of creatures. Of himself or herself, a person does not have the capacity and strength to deal with such an experience, for here the person faces God filled with the graces of all creatures, awesome in power, glory, and excellence. However, such a person no longer fears, for God acts in a friendly way towards him or her. God reveals divine power with love and goodness. God communicates strength and love, admirable virtues, charity, knowledge of higher and lower substances, and transforms a person with the attributes of God.

Here God dwells within a person with an embrace that is close, intimate, interior, and pure. The person experiences this intimate embrace sometimes in enjoying God in quiet passivity, sometimes in an awakening when God communicates knowledge and love. Such a person should withdraw from all business matters and live in immense tranquility, so that nothing may disturb the union with the Beloved. However, in the person striving to be perfect all is perfect, and the awakening and in-breathing of the Holy Spirit is strangely delightful. God breathes the Holy Spirit into the person and produces an awakening of divine knowledge, thus absorbing that one in God and rousing love. This breathing of the Holy Spirit fills the person with good and glory and enkindles him or her in love of God, to whom be honor and glory forever and ever. Amen.

Reflections on stanza four

The entire poem celebrates the divine gifts communicated to a person in spiritual marriage. In this fourth stanza the person is overwhelmed with deep love and thanks God for two gifts in particular that manifest the indwelling of God. The first is an awakening of God in the person that leads him or her to a totally new vision of reality, and the second is an overflowing of God's love that makes it seem as if God is now breathing in the person. This is a stanza of peace and gratitude. Instead of bursting forth in song, as in the previous verses, here the person quietly celebrates the fullness of life experienced in this transformation.

We use the term awakening on a personal and on a group level. It implies coming to life in a new way, with a new awareness. We speaks of the awakening of a conversion, or we speak about a cultural, national, value based awakening. In this stanza the awakening refers to a newly gained awareness that love is the central value of life. Generally people become captivated to the new awareness and live differently after the awakening. John tells us that this awakening is felt in the very substance of the person, giving awareness of all the grace-filled wonders of the world and of every creature in perfect harmony. All the creatures of the world "disclose the beauties of their being, power, loveliness, and graces, . . . For the soul is conscious of how all creatures, earthly and heavenly, have their life, duration, and strength in Him" (F. 4.5). The person sees clearly how all creatures are distinct from God, but how they all can be understood better when viewed as part of God's being than in themselves. "And here lies the remarkable delight of this awakening: the soul knows creatures through God and not God through creatures" (F. 4.5). This is God's gift to the person, a totally new vision of reality; the revelation of the newness and harmony of the world in God. In this gift, the person is awakened from a natural vision to a supernatural vision (F. 4.6). He or she, free from the veils that covered true sight, now sees both God and God-in-creatures in one moment's vision. It is like an awakening from sleep, achieved by the power of God's love within us. It is an awakening of God's excellence and power in the person's inner substance; an awakening so overwhelming that a person could not endure it had he or she not already gone through purification and had not God communicated this vision with friendliness, gentleness, and love. "Thus the soul experiences in Him as much gentleness and love as it does power and dominion and grandeur" (F. 4.12).

This communication of a vision of the cosmos in God is given in the depths of the person, where God dwells in secret. The more a person has been purified the more God dwells within, feeling at home there, and the more the person longs to be alone with God, away from all other interests. In this awakening the person feels delight in experiencing God so present it seems God is breathing within it. "And in that awakening, which is as though one were to awaken and breathe. The soul feels a strange delight in the breathing of the Holy Spirit in God" (F. 4.16). In this awakening of knowledge of God and the cosmos, a person finds that it is now the Holy Spirit who breathes new life within him or her, filling the person with good and glory and enkindling him or her in love for God, "indescribably and incomprehensibly" (F. 4.17). Breath is life and without it we die. Sometimes a person who seems to be dying can receive artificial respiration and gain life again because someone breathes air into them. Sometimes people who have lost the ability to breathe on their own need to use a respirator. In this case God breathes new life into us and gives us chance to live in a new way we never expected.

Key concepts

"The soul knows creatures through God and not God through creatures" (F. 4.5).

John loved the beauty of God's creation not just in general but with a particular appreciation for each one of God's creatures (las criaturas). There are four points to John's approach to creation. First, the temporal veil of all creatures must be renounced if one is to seek union with God. Creatures, in spite of their beauty, cannot become ends in themselves. "[I]n order to obtain union with God. . . all the things of the world are renounced, all natural appetites and affections mortified" (F. 1.29). John is not opposed to nature, but knows it can become a block to union with God when people are attached and possessive of things. "If you purify your soul of attachments and desires, you will understand things spiritually. If you deny your appetite for them, you will enjoy their truth, understanding what is certain in them" (S. 49). At first, the person actively participates in this purification, but later it is achieved by the transforming love of the Trinity. "You detach and withdraw the soul from all the other touches of created things by the might of Your delicacy, and reserve it for and unite it to Yourself alone" (F. 2.18).

The second point in John's approach is to appreciate that during the ascetical period of the spiritual journey creatures can lead one to God, for "the consideration of creatures is first in order after the exercise of self-knowledge" (C. 4.1). This is important for it helps us appreciate the greatness of God's love and generosity in creation and can thus awaken our love for God. "Only the hand of God, her Beloved, was able to create this diversity and grandeur" (C. 4.3). When John looks at the world in this way he concludes, "It seems to (the soul) that the entire universe is a sea of love in which it is engulfed, for, conscious of the living point or center of love within itself, it is unable to catch sight of the boundaries of this love" (F. 2.10).

The third point in John's approach is when in contemplation all is transformed in God in spiritual betrothal and a person sees God in every aspect of creation. "In that nocturnal tranquility and silence and in the knowledge of the divine light the soul becomes aware of Wisdom's wonderful harmony and sequence in the variety of her creatures and works" (C. 14-15.25). John helps us discover the inner world of God's love, and in the *Spiritual Canticle* he represents "a reordering of the cosmos, a world made new," and "we begin to see that world differently and sense something of its beauty and wonder."[19] Earlier in the spiritual journey creation was a reflection of God's beauty, later reflection moves to identification, "My Beloved, the mountains. . ."

At first, a reader can easily feel disoriented when reading John's forceful opposition to all created things, and then see his love and enthusiasm for the same. However, John has several examples of pursuing two seemingly opposing concepts at the same time.[20] We must take John's positions within the context of his theological and spiritual vision of life. Clearly, he opposes anything that is not God, and if creatures lead one away from God then any attachment to them must be opposed. On the other hand John focuses less on detachment than on integration; he wants a person to give absolutely every aspect of life to God. After purification and transformation, a person sees how all created things are integral to God's vision of love. "[I]n the living contemplation and knowledge of creatures the soul sees such fullness of graces, powers, and beauty with which God has endowed them that seemingly all are arranged in wonderful beauty and natural virtue" (C. 6.1). So, John quotes St. Francis' statement that now God and everything are his, and in the "Prayer of a soul taken with love" he claims that every aspect of creation is now his in union with God.

John's steps from renunciation to seeing reflections of God's beauty in creation, to an appreciation of the sacramental quality of creation, and moves on in the *Living Flame* to a wonderful conclusion, his fourth point; that a person knows creatures through God and not God through creatures. At this time a person experiences an awakening of the Word in the deepest part of his or her spirit, so that "all the virtues and substances and perfections and graces of every created thing glow and make the same movement all at once" (F. 4.4). Thus, "all things seem to move in unison," and "they all likewise disclose the beauties of their being, power, loveliness, and graces, and the root of their duration and life. For the soul is conscious of how all creatures, earthly and heavenly, have their life, duration, and strength in Him" (F 4.5).

John offers a wonderful conclusion, namely, that a person now knows all these created things better in God's being than in themselves. "And here lies the remarkable delight of this awakening: the soul knows creatures through God and not God through creatures" (F. 4.5). This is a reversal of our normal ways of thinking about these things: we know the effects through the cause and not the cause through the effects. This is a new supernatural vision of the relationship between God and creation. In this vision, a person "sees what God is in Himself and what He is in His creatures in only one view" (F. 4.7). This is a mystical vision of the cosmos, in which every creature has its place and meaning in the plan of God, for all creation is restored in God's transforming love.

All creatures are so united to God that they become divine while preserving their own independent existence. In the dialogue between the Father and the Son in the third "Romance" the Father gives the world to the Son as a bride. The Son replies, "I will hold her in my arms and she will burn with your love and with eternal delight she will exalt your goodness." The Son's spiritual marriage with creation becomes part of the project of love between the Father and the Son, and we can now see creation as God does. The fourth stanza of the *Living Flame* gives us an appreciation of the whole world as sharing in the glory of God, and the love we now find in the world is the epiphany of God's love.

Awakening to a new vision (see F. 4.2).

In stanza four of the *Living Flame* the person in spiritual marriage celebrates God's actions within him or her that awaken the person to a completely new vision of reality. Yet again John disrupts our way of thinking and understanding of God's role in our lives. Something happens under the transforming power of God's love that opens the way to a new vision of God and of a new transformed humanity. This includes awareness that God always remains the same but always renews all things. John calls this "an awakening of God in the soul, brought about in gentleness and love" (F. 4.2).

This awakening takes place in the center and depth of a person where God dwells. It is "a movement of the Word in the substance of the soul" (F. 4.4). Again, he says "this awakening is the communication of God's excellence to the substance of the soul" (F. 4.10). When John speaks about substance he refers to the most interior point within the human spirit where a person enjoys the fruits of union with God. John says God dwells in a person's heart in secret, and remains hidden in the very substance of a person's soul. Here, the power of God's love causes this awakening. It is the transformation of one's vision of world reality.

In this awakening, the person experiences the power of the Son of God who captivates a person in love. In this encounter a person realizes vitally what both John the evangelist and Paul in *Acts* declared; "in him is life," and "In him we live and move and have our being." In this awakening, a person sees everything integrated into a unified vision of God in which all creatures "disclose the beauties of their being, power, loveliness, and graces, and the root of their duration and life" (F. 4.5). The person becomes conscious of how all creatures find their meaning only in God, and he or she sees the whole world in one unified vision of God. In this vision of total harmony of the cosmos in the power and love of God, a person appreciates how God moves, sustains, and governs the universe, bestowing being, power, and grace all on creatures. This awakening, this contemplative glance of reality changes everything.

John says that in this awakening a person arises from the sleep of a natural vision to a supernatural vision. In this last stage of spiritual marriage, God peels away some of the many veils that block perception of the spiritual vision of reality. "[T]he soul. . . is renewed and moved by God so that it might behold this supernatural sight. . . that divine life and the being and harmony of every creature in that life, with its movements in God, is revealed to it with such newness" (F. 4.6). As God does this a person begins to see the entire plan of God's love for the world and God's strategy of love for humanity. Even while commenting on stanza one, John pointed out that a person now "has God's view of things, he regards them as God does" (F. 1.32). No wonder John says this vision captivates him and arouses a response of deeper love for God (F. 4. 3). Having seen this vision, he goes on to conclude stanza four and the entire poem of the *Living Flame* with the beautiful awareness, "How tenderly You swell my heart with love!" The poem and the experience it describes end in complete peace and union.

CONCLUSION
SIX CHALLENGES FOR OUR DAILY LIVES

*T*he *Living Flame of Love* may well be beyond our understanding and experience, but it is without a doubt one of the greatest spiritual books of world history. One thing is clear; if we are interested in the spiritual life then we have to read the *Living Flame of Love*. It is a must! We may be outside that circle of people who understand it from experience, but we can appreciate it at least a little from outside the circle and remain in wonder and awe at its message and call. Let us conclude our study of the *Living Flame* with six challenges for our daily lives.

Now and again, let us look back at where we came from.

"From darkness to darkness, guided by that darkness" (F. 3.71).

We live today in dark times. Throughout the *Living Flame* John often looks back, and in one of his digressions he reminds us that before God's illumination we were once obscure and blind. "God is the light and the object of the soul, and when this light does not illumine it, the soul dwells in obscurity even though it may have very excellent vision" (F. 3.70). At that time we were incapable of even desiring the transformation of which the *Living Flame* speaks, and were content to live in the darkness we knew so well. John summarizes how things were when he says we went from darkness to darkness, guided by that darkness. No matter our dedication, it often seems we just cannot see things in the way God sees things or in the way God wants us to see things. John says we live with cataracts that cover the spiritual eyes! Anyone who has had cataract surgery will acknowledge the brilliance of this example. Whatever you look at you see through the cataract—it puts a filter over everything. In fact you get to the point where you begin to think that what you see is all there is to see! In this situation, the problem is that "one will infallibly come to consider the things of God as impertinent to God, and the things impertinent to God as belonging to God" (F. 3.73).

The *Living Flame* reminds us how God drew us out of this darkness. From time to time it is worth remembering where we were, for the joy of coming into the light is never as great as when you have been in darkness.[21] God leads us out of this darkness, through the pains of purification and the illumination of contemplation. God guides us by the hand and trains us see in a new way.

Let us allow the Living Flame's vision of love condition all we do:

"The soul perceives clearly that love is proper to eternal life" (F. 3.5).

John teaches us that love is the very reason why we were created (C. 29.3), the ultimate reason for everything in life (C. 38.5), and that at the end of life we will be judged on love (S. 60). The *Living Flame* teaches us about the priority of love in every aspect of life. However, John's teaching gives an unusual and contemporary focus to our understanding of the nature of love. God reveals love in the communication of divine attributes. God loves with the full force of each of the attributes and with all of them influencing each other.[22] Thus, God loves with justice, goodness, mercy, and so on. "Each lamp burns in love, and the warmth from each furthers the warmth of the other, and the flame of one the flame of the other, because through each attribute the other is known" (F. 3.5). This becomes one of the richest explanations of love in the whole of spiritual literature.

The person seeking union discovers that God's personal love for him or her is imbued with every one of the attributes. The person thus sees that "love is proper to eternal life." However, it is also a very clear project of action for Christians in their ministries throughout the world. So, each of these qualities becomes a lamp illuminating all apostolic action and at the same time casts a protective shadow over love that assures its authenticity.

We can describe the spiritual journey in several ways, but included among them is the understanding that our journey to God is the gradual acquisition and understanding of the nature of love. As we journey to God we perceive that love is the essential component of life. It is who God is and it is our own goal in life.

We must accept that our role in the spiritual journey is to receive.

The person accomplishes a lot by learning to do nothing (F. 3.47).

The *Living Flame* reminds us over and over again that God is the agent of all spiritual growth. God is the principal lover in leading us along the road to union; "He acts as the blind man's guide who must lead it by the hand to the place it does not know how to reach" (F. 3.29). No matter how much we think we are seeking God, it is always God who takes the initiative in seeking us. Our responsibility is to place no obstacles in the way of progress. In the spiritual life there should be no dabbling, experimenting here and there with various systems and practices. We must be single-minded in our commitment, persevere in a chosen way, and need to prepare ourselves to receive. God does all the work. In his digressions, John urges his disciples to learn the importance of passivity and receptivity. When speaking of spiritual marriage in the *Spiritual Canticle* he says that when the soul is "won over to love," she even withdraws from active life to focus exclusively on "the attentiveness of love towards God." He then speaks about "solitary love . . . the end for which we were created," and refers to this as "holy idleness." He tells us that a person "having reached the intimate love of God . . . considers everything else of little consequence" (C. 29). While John is firm on the priority to be given to solitary love and union with God, we should also remember that John was very active in dedicated ministry as his own mystical union gave rise to intense apostolic activity in the service of others.

Sometimes it seems in our desire for spiritual growth that we are running out of time. We are not! There is lots of time if we have the right perspective and realize it is God who is acting within us. If a person is willing to leave aside his or her own natural ways of acting and place self in a receptive attitude towards God, then God places that person "in solitude and in the state of listening." Such a person should enter "this simple and idle state of contemplation," "this idle tranquility," with a spirit that is silent and detached. Lest we think we are not doing our part, John comments; "Even though the soul is not then doing anything, God is doing something in it" (F. 3.46). "I shall prove to you that it is accomplishing a great deal by doing nothing" (F. 3.47). He then comments on how a person does a lot by not working with intellect, memory, and will, adding that "God introduces [the soul] into that emptiness and solitude where it is unable to use the faculties" (F. 3.66).

We often think we advance by our own willpower and efforts, purifying sense activities to earn a spiritual approach. John requires the purification of sense, but then insists it is God's love that leads a person to a life of the spirit and that overflows and transforms sense. Although we read it is best to do nothing, the texts really mean it is best to do nothing except to love God and neighbor. Nothing else is important. "It is sufficient for it [the soul] to possess one degree of love, for by one degree alone it is united with Him through grace" (F. 1.13; see also S. 12).

May our understanding of God influence all we do.

"The soul perceives the power of the other life" (F. 1.32).

God communicates the abundant enrichment of union. A person drawn to this union perceives the weaknesses of this life and the power of the other life. A spiritual person always lives on two planes of existence; he or she lives in the here and now while at the same time living elsewhere. But the "here and now" is conditioned by the "there and then." There are two horizons of life, this one and a horizon of life beyond this one that gives meaning to this one. Every human being now and again catches a glimpse of the life beyond this one, and this becomes the foundation for faith. However, the *Living Flame* presents us with a powerful vision of the "there and then" that impacts all we do in the "here and now." John says that only a very thin veil separates us from the life of the world beyond this one. This changes the way a person views this world and its values. "And this life is even much less in the eyes of a person thus exalted, for, since he has God's view of things, he regards them as God does" (F. 1.32).

There is no more important a question for anyone seeking God than to ask what happens at death. The person in the *Living Flame* longs so much for union that he or she wants God to break through the veil of death. The life beyond this one that gives meaning to this one, influences all of us in the way we live in this world while yearning for the world beyond this one. This is a new level of consciousness. A person sees the power of God to transform his or her life, appreciates that God is the principal actor, and realizes that growth and readiness for the next life is the result of God's work within us. So, while a person longs for union, he or she is primarily concerned to accept God's will for life or death.

May the communication of divine attributes transform all life.

By his image alone he clothed us in beauty (see C. stanza 5).

Transformation takes place in spiritual marriage and continues in eternity through deeper union and the revelation of the divine mysteries. God brings about this transformation in a person in contemplation, after the person becomes receptive to God's activity. From the earliest stages, this communication is always a transformation in love (C. 1.10; 7.4; 13.1). The *Living Flame* presents the final transformative action of God in the person prior to the transfer from this life to the next. John calls this "abundant and lofty knowledge of God," "illumination and the warmth of love," and a revelation of the unique and simple being of God. What God reveals at this final stage of spiritual marriage is that God is in essence and simplicity of being all the powers of the divine attributes. This is not information but a disclosure of the nature of God by experiencing the full force of each and all the attributes. In this experience the person is transformed by and into the power of the attributes. "Since each of these attributes is the very being of God in His one and only *suppositum*, which is the Father, the Son, and the Holy Spirit, and since each one is God in Himself, Who is infinite light or divine fire, we deduce that the soul, like God gives forth light and warmth through each of these innumerable attributes" (F. 3.2).

Many people spend their lives affirming statements about who they think God is, and often this has very little impact on their lives, even on the lives of the very dedicated. John, on the other hand, tells us that God acts towards us and in us with the full power of each and every one of the divine attributes. Moreover, he tells us that each attribute cannot be understood separated from love, for God loves with the full force of each attribute. "The light communicated to it from all these attributes together is enveloped in the warmth of the love of God by which it loves Him because He is all these things" (F. 3.3). In appreciating this divine communication and transformation, it is appropriate that we apply to ourselves what John said about creation in the *Spiritual Canticle*; "And having looked at them, with his image alone, clothed them in beauty" (stanza 5).

May the end draw us to journey with enthusiasm.

"The soul abounds in delights" (see F. 2.21).

John tells us that a person's experience of God is indescribable and that it touches the very inner substance of a person. It is a taste of eternal life and "pays every debt," tribulation, trial, or penance a person has undergone to get to this point (F. 2.23). John points out that sometime the experience is so profound that it overflows into an experience the body shares. He calls it "the rapture of love" (F. 3.5) and says that in this experience a person understands that love is of the essence of everything significant in life. John gives us four aspects of this experience. First, a person is united in love with the Holy Spirit. Second, he or she is immersed in the life and love of the Holy Trinity. Third, the person is transformed by the love and attributes of God. Fourth, the person gains a new vision of the entire cosmos in union with the Word, the Son of God. John says several times that he feels he cannot do justice to describing how wonderful this experience is. "The appropriate language for the person receiving these favors is that he understand them, experience them within himself, enjoy them, and be silent" (F. 2.21).

The purpose and destiny of each of us is to be in union with God in love in eternity. Everything else is secondary. Most of us will end up taking the broad valleys of earthly and heavenly goods that John describes in his diagram of Mount Carmel. Many of us will make the journey long, laborious, and only partially successful in attaining the goal. In the *Living Flame* John shows us the end of the journey and in his digressions reminds us and encourages us to take the shortcut of the direct, but steep and narrow way, to the top of Mount Carmel. His descriptions in the *Living Flame* are so powerful and awesome that they become motivation for each of us to undertake this journey with enthusiasm. We will always be restless until we reach the goal for which we were created.

NOTES

1. Xavier Pikaza, "Amore de Dios y contemplación crisitana: Introducción a San Juan de la Cruz." *Actas III*, p. 53.

2. For further developments on this theme within the context of a vision of love, see my book, *The One Thing Necessary: The Transforming Power of Christian Love* (Chicago: ACTA Publications, 2012).

3. See my book, *The Dark Night Is Our Only Light: A Study of the Book of the Dark Night by John of the Cross*, chapter 6, "Seeing the world through the lens of love."

4. See my book, *John of the Cross—The Spiritual Canticle: The Encounter of Two Lovers*, 2013, "The Soul's Experience of God's Transforming Presence," pp. 192-197.

5. For details on John's many directees, see my book, *John of the Cross: Your Spiritual Guide*, pp. 20-21

6. See my book, *The Dark Night is Our Only Light*, pp. 26-29: "The Environment in Which John Lived."

7. Fr. Gabriel of St. Mary Magdalen, *St. John of the Cross: Doctor of Divine Love and Contemplation* (Westminster, MD: The Newman Press, 1954), p. 81.

8. See Bernard Giovate, *San Juan de la Cruz* (New York: Twayne Publishers, Inc. 1971): chapter 6, "The Revelation of Poetry." Regarding the *Living Flame*, Brenan comments; "[H]e took the form of the stanzas from the opening to Garcilasco's Canción Segunda, where it figures as a semi-strophe. The first line, *Oh llama de amore viva*, would seem to have been suggested by a line from Sebastián de Córdoba's pastiche of Garcilasco, which runs *El fuego de amor vivo*, and there are three other borrowings from Garcilasco in it." Gerald Brenan, *The Literature of the Spanish People* (Harmondsworth: Penguin, 1963), pp. 126-127.

9. Fr. Federico Ruiz Salvador, one of the greatest recent exponents of the works of John of the Cross, insists this is deliberate on John's part. He suggests that this is a way in which John's poetry reflects his mystical experience. John complements this technique of adding richness and fullness to the experience by his use of exclamations that create a sense of wonder. See Federico Ruiz Salvador, *Introducción a San Juan de la Cruz* (Madrid: Biblioteca de Autores Christianos, 1968), p. 254.

10. Colin Thompson, *St. John of the Cross: Songs in the Night* (Washington, DC: Catholic University Press of America, 2003), p. 277.

11. E. Allison Peers, *St. John of the Cross: Living Flame of Love* (New York: Image Books, 1962), p.9.

12. Thompson, 273-274.

13. See chapter 3 of my book, *The Dark Night is Our Only Light.*

14. "The substance is that capacity or faculty in one's psychological makeup for experiencing fruition, delight, and joy; or sadness, anguish, and desolation, etc. . . . Just as the union in the intellect is faith (knowledge) and the union in the will is charity (love), so the union in the substance of the soul is fruition, peace, and so on; it is intense in the actual transient union, and subdued, although sometimes profound, in the habitual union." *The Collected Works of St. John of the Cross*, Translated by Kieran Kavanaugh, OCD. And Otilio Rodriguez, OCD. (Washington, DC: ICS Publications, 1979), p. 572-3. See also John Welch, *When Gods Die: An Introduction to John of the Cross.* New York/Mahwah: Paulist Press, 1990), p. 57: "John sometimes speaks of a point of interiority within the human spirit which he refers to as the substance."

15. In the *Spiritual Canticle*, 38 and 39, John says that the transformation includes experiencing the "what," the indescribable. He includes the following characteristics of the "what." 1. Spiration of the Holy Spirit from the God to the bride, and from her to God. 2. Jubilation in fruition of God. 3. Knowledge of creatures in their harmony. 4. Pure and clear contemplation of the divine essence. 5. Total transformation in love of God.

16. Welch, p. 63.

17. Welch, p. 145.

18. John describes the feeling that the Living Flame causes in the person. "O enkindled love, with your loving movements you are pleasantly glorifying me according to the greater capacity and strength of my soul, bestowing divine

knowledge according to all the ability and capacity of my intellect, and communicating love according the greater power of my will, and rejoicing the substance of my soul with the torrent of your delight by your divine contact and substantial union, in harmony with the greater purity of my substance and the capacity and breadth of my memory" (F. 1.17).

19. Thompson, p. 277.

20. See my book, *John of the Cross: Your Spiritual Guide*, chapter 6, pp. 80-89, where I list the following double-attitudes: patience-urgency, perseverance-flexibility, detachment-integration, fortitude-emptiness, personal solitude-community, live here-live elsewhere, and all-nothing.

21. See Isaiah 42:16. "I will lead the blind by a road they do not know, by paths they have not known I will guide them. I will turn the darkness before them into light, the rough places into level ground. These are the things I will do, and I will not forsake them."

22. Speaking of God John says; "Since He is omnipotent, He omnipotently loves and does good to you; since He is wise, you feel that He loves and does good to you with wisdom; since He is infinitely good, you feel that He loves you with goodness; since He is holy, you feel that with holiness He loves and favors you; since He is just, you feel that in justice He loves and favors you; since He is merciful, mild, and clement, you feel his mercy, mildness, and clemency; since He is a strong, sublime, and delicate being, you feel that His love for you is strong, sublime, and delicate; since He is pure and undefiled, you feel that He loves you in a pure and undefiled way; since He is truth, you feel that He loves you in truthfulness; since He is liberal, you feel that He liberally loves and favors you, without any personal profit, only in order to do good to you; since He is the virtue of supreme humility, He loves you with supreme humility and esteem and makes you His equal, gladly revealing Himself to you in these ways of knowledge. . . ." (F. 3.6).

BIBLIOGRAPHY

Brenan, Gerald. *The Literature of the Spanish People*. Penguin: Harmondsworth, 1963.

Brenan, Gerald. *St John of the Cross: His Life and Poetry*. Cambridge, England: Cambridge University Press, 1973.

de Cordoba, Sebastián. *Love of God for the Soul*. 1575.

Doohan, Leonard. *The Contemporary Challenge of John of the Cross*. Washington, DC: ICS Publications, 1995.

Doohan, Leonard. *The One Thing Necessary: The Transforming Power of Christian Love*. Chicago: ACTA Publications, 2012.

Doohan, Leonard. *The Dark Night is Our Only Light: A study of the book of the Dark Night by John of the Cross*. 2013.

Doohan Leonard. *John of the Cross: Your Spiritual Guide.* 2013.

Doohan, Leonard. *John of the Cross—The Spiritual Canticle: The Encounter of Two Lovers*. 2013.

Fr. Gabriel of St. Mary Magdalen. *St. John of the Cross: Doctor of Divine Love and Contemplation*. Westminster, MD: The Newman Press, 1954.

Bernard Giovate, *San Juan de la Cruz.* New York: Twayne
Publishers, Inc. 1971.

Peers, E. Allison. *St. John of the Cross: The Living Flame of
Love.* New York: Image Books, 1962.

Pikaza, Xavier. "Amore de Dios y contemplación crisitana:
Introducción a San Juan de la Cruz." *Actas III.* 51-96.

Ruiz Salvador, Federico. *Introducción a San Juan de la Cruz.*
Madrid: Biblioteca de Autores Cristianos, 1968.

Thompson, Colin. *St. John of the Cross: Songs in the Night.*
Washington, DC: Catholic University Press of America,
2003.

Welch, John. *When Gods Die: An Introduction to John of the
Cross.* New York/Mahwah: Paulist Press, 1990.

BOOKS AND E-BOOKS

A Year with St. John of the Cross: 365 Daily Readings and Reflections

This book, *A Year with St. John of the Cross*, offers 365 daily readings and reflection. In this year with St. John of the Cross we will read and reflect on his life, ministry, spiritual direction, spirituality, as well as selections from all his works, short and long. The readings and reflections in this book will introduce readers to all these, as well as comments from many leading writers and commentators on John. This year will be an opportunity for readers to immerse themselves in the spirituality of John of the Cross. Each day offers a focused reading, four key reflections, and three specific challenges for the day.

For those who are enthusiastic supporters of St. John of the Cross, and for others who wish to discover new and substantial paths in their spiritual journey, this book is a one-of-a-kind opportunity to encounter John and his challenges like never before. Let your reading of this new book be your personal journey with John of the Cross, to a deeper union with God. One of the main uses of the book is to help readers who do not have ready access to a spiritual director. Maybe these readings and reflections will help. I hope you will find this special book helpful in your spiritual journey.

"Thank you so much for the excellent work. Your insights and reflection questions are wonderful."

"The clarity of the book, along with its depth without being complex, makes this work a real treasure."

"What a great idea and a superb execution, a work that will be helpful to so many."

"I recently purchased the Kindle edition of your book on St. John of the Cross. I have been reading from it each day as part of my prayer time. To sum it up in a word: wow!"

THE CONTEMPORARY CHALLENGE OF JOHN OF THE CROSS

STUDIES OF THE MAJOR WORKS OF JOHN OF THE CROSS

This series presents introductions to each of the great works of John of the Cross. Each volume is a study guide to one of John's major works and gives all the necessary background for anyone who wishes to approach this great spiritual writer with appropriate preparation in order to reap the benefits of one of the most challenging figures in the history of spirituality. Each book is a complete introduction offering background, history, knowledge, insight, and theological and spiritual analysis for anyone who wishes to immerse himself or herself into the spiritual vision of John of the Cross.

While targeted to the general reader these volumes would be helpful to anyone who is interested in the spiritual guidance of this saint. These books give insight into the critical components of spiritual life and can be helpful for anyone interested in his or her own spiritual journey. They could be helpful for the many people involved in the spiritual guidance of others, whether in spiritual direction, retreat work, chaplaincy, and other such ministries. Throughout these books the reader is encouraged to develop the necessary attitudes, enthusiasm, spiritual sensitivity, and contemplative spirit needed to benefit from these spiritual masterpieces of John of the Cross. Attentive reflection on these studies will encourage readers to have a genuine love for John of the Cross and his approach to the spiritual journey.

These books give historical, regional, and religious background rarely found in other introductory books on John of the Cross. They each present an abbreviated and accessible form of John's great works. Later chapters in each book give John's theological and spiritual insights that could be used for personal reflection and group discussion. Sections abound in quotes and references from John's books and each sub-section can be used as the basis for daily meditation. The volumes complement each other, and together give the reader excellent foundation for reading the works of this great spiritual leader and saint.

Volume 1. John of the Cross: Your Spiritual Guide

This unique book is written as if John of the Cross is speaking directly to the reader. It is a presentation by John of the Cross of seven sessions to a reader who has expressed interest in John's life and teachings. This book introduces the great mystic and his teachings to his reader and to all individuals who yearn for a deeper commitment in their spiritual lives and consider that John could be the person who can guide them.

Table of contents

1. John's life as a contemporary life
2. John as a spiritual guide
3. John's vision of the spiritual life
4. Preparations for the spiritual journey
5. Major moments and decisions in the spiritual life
6. Necessary attitudes during the spiritual journey
7. Celebrating the goal of the spiritual journey

Volume 2. The Dark Night is Our Only Light: A study of the book of the *Dark Night* by John of the Cross

This introduction to the *Dark Night of the Soul* by John of the Cross gives all the necessary background for anyone who wishes to approach this great spiritual work with appropriate preparation in order to reap the benefits of one of the most challenging works in the history of spirituality. The book starts with the life of John of the Cross, identifying the dark nights of his own life. It provides the needed historical, religious, and personal background to appreciate and locate its content. It then presents readers with aids they can use to understand the work. With these preparations in mind the book moves on to present the stages of the spiritual life and the importance of the nights. A summary of John's own work brings readers in direct contact with the challenges of the message and its application today. The book ends with 20 key questions that often arise when someone reads this book.

Table of contents

1. John of the Cross and the dark nights of his own life
2. Influences on John's writing of the *Dark Night*
3. Aids to reading the *Dark Night*
4. Understanding the book of the *Dark Night*
5. The book of the *Dark Night* by John of the Cross – a summary
6. Five key spiritual challenges of the book of the *Dark Night*
7. The dark night in contemporary life
8. Twenty questions for John of the Cross and his book of the *Dark Night*

Volume 3. The Spiritual Canticle: The Encounter of Two Lovers. An introduction to the book of the *Spiritual Canticle* by John of the Cross

The book starts with the life of John of the Cross, showing how he was always a model of love in his own life, and how, guided by his own experience he became a teacher and later a poet of human and divine love. The book provides the needed historical, religious, and personal background to appreciate and locate its content. The book then presents the links between John's *Spiritual Canticle* and Scripture's love poem, the *Song of Songs*. A summary of John's own work brings readers in direct contact with the challenges of the message and its application today. With these preparations in mind the book moves on to present the stages of the spiritual life and the importance of the journey of love. The book then focuses on key concepts in the *Spiritual Canticle*, applying each of them to contemporary situations. Finally it considers the images of God presented in the book and how they relate to the spiritual journey.

Table of contents

Volume 4. John of the Cross: The Living Flame of Love

The *Living Flame of Love* is the final chapter in John's vision of love. It describes the end of a journey that began in longings of love that became an experience of purification for the person seeking union. *The Living Flame of Love* picks up from the final stage of union in the love of spiritual marriage and describes, in great beauty, several aspects of this final stage in the union of love. All these ideas are part of John's wonderful vision of love. Many writers have emphasized the spiritual value of a life of love, but John's vision is more expansive and integrated than approaches presented by anyone else.

Table of contents

The Contemporary Challenge of St. Teresa of Avila

An Introduction to her life and teachings

This book is an introduction to the life and teachings of St. Teresa of Avila. It is a collection of notes and reflections taken from material I have presented in courses and workshops on St. Teresa over many years and in many countries to people from all walks of life who see Teresa's teachings on prayer as the vision and guidance they long for. This book on *The Contemporary Challenge of Saint Teresa of Avila*, is an introduction to her life and writings, and readers should use it as a companion to the careful and prayerful reading of Teresa's own writings. It is in no way a substitute for reading her works, in fact I have rarely quoted from her writings, insisting that readers must encounter them for themselves. I hope these notes and reflections will introduce readers to this giant in the history of spirituality and one of the greatest teachers of prayer that the world has ever known. This book is a companion to an earlier book, *The Contemporary Challenge of St. John of the Cross*, which was used extensively by individuals and groups as an introduction to St. John of the Cross' life and teachings. It was also used by many in formation programs. This current book on Teresa may well fulfill similar goals.

MORE BOOKS ON CONTEMPORARY SPIRITUALITY FOR CHRISTIAN ADULTS

The One Thing Necessary: The Transforming Power of Christian Love.

This radical new interpretation of love as the touchstone of the Christian message, explores the human longing for meaning; the Scriptures; the relational model of the Trinity: the ideas of human vocation, destiny and community; the mystical spiritual traditions; and his own experiences to explain what love is, how we find it, and how it can change the world. Each of the seven chapters contains several quotes and focus points at the beginning and provocative questions at the end for reflection or discussion by adult religious education and bible study groups.

"This book is all about love—and love as the one thing necessary. It is most certainly not about easy love or cheap grace. It is about the transforming power of Christian love. It is not only challenging but disturbing, a book written with conviction and passion." **Fr. Wilfrid Harrington, OP.**, Biblical scholar.

"[Doohan's] artful gathering and arranging of ideas reminds one of the impact of a gigantic bouquet of mixed flowers chosen individually and with great care." **Carol Blank**, *Top 1000 reviewers, USA.*

"Would that we heard more about this in our churches and religious discussions because, "this transforming power of Christian love will save the world" (p. 93). **Mary S. Sheridan**, *"Spirit and Life."*

The One Thing Necessary: The Transforming Power of Christian Love is available from www.actapublications.com or from amazon.com

Rediscovering Jesus' Priorities

This book urges readers to look again at Jesus' teachings and identify the major priorities. It is a call to rethink the essential components of a living and vital Christianity and a challenge to rediscover the basic values Jesus proclaimed. Use the book for a short meditation and personal examination, as a self-guided retreat to call yourself to renewed dedication to Jesus' call, or for group discussion and renewed application of Jesus' teachings.

Ten Strategies to Nurture Our Spiritual Lives: Don't stand still—nurture the life within you

This book presents ten key steps or strategies to support and express the faith of those individuals who seek to deepen their spirituality through personal commitment and group growth. These ten key components of spirituality enable dedicated adults to bring out the meaning of their faith and to facilitate their spiritual growth. It offers a program of reflection, discussion, planning, journaling, strategizing, and sharing.

How to Become a Great Spiritual Leader: Ten Steps and a Hundred Suggestions

This is a book for daily meditation. It has a single focus—how to become a great spiritual leader. It is a book on the spirituality of a leader's personal life. It presumes that leadership is a vocation, and that it results from an inner transformation. The book proposes ten steps that individuals can take to enable this process of transformation, and a hundred suggestions to make this transformation real and lasting. It is a unique book in the literature on leadership.

This book is the third in a series on leadership. The first, *Spiritual Leadership: The Quest for Integrity* gave the foundations of leadership today. The second, *Courageous Hope: The Call of Leadership*, gave the contemporary characteristics and qualities of leadership. This third book focuses on the spirituality of the leader.

Courageous Hope: The Call of Leadership

This book's focus on leadership and hope is very appropriate given today's climate of distrust that many find results in a sense of hopelessness in their current leaders. Individuals and organizations are desperate for leaders of hope. Many books on leadership point to the need for inner motivation, but that inner motivation must be hope in new possibilities for a changed future. It is hope that gives a meaningful expression to leadership and enables the leader to be creative in dealing with the present. More than anything else it is a vision of hope that can excite and empower leaders to inspire others to strive for a common vision.

ALL BOOKS ARE AVAILABLE FROM AMAZON.COM

Readers interested in John of the Cross
can participate in the author's blog
johnofthecrosstoday.wordpress.com

Visit the author's webpage at
leonarddoohan.com

Made in the USA
San Bernardino, CA
10 December 2016

42886200R00102